The Gospel Centered Worship Leader

Credits:

JT Cheek - Cover Design
Mark Steele - Editor
Janetta Oni - Layout

A thirteen week study for discipling worship leaders

4

Acknowledgments

Wow! This book has literally been in the making for about 10 years now. I have only been aware of it for the past year, but all along God has been using my experiences, opportunities, weaknesses, and failures to begin teaching me so that one day, I may in turn teach others. Well, I guess that day is now and while I still don't have it all figured out, I am grateful to the Lord for being patient with me and teaching me as I go.

There are many people who have been very instrumental in seeing this book become a reality and I would like to take a moment to acknowledge them.

First, I would like to thank David Rogers who is not just my Pastor, but also a spiritual giant to me and has supported me and believed in me since we first met. I have learned so much from you and will continue to learn what it means to passionately love God and serve Him with all your heart, soul, mind, and strength. I feel as though this book should have you as the co-author because almost everything in here has been learned from you. Thank you for giving me a chance.

I would also like to thank my family. Mom and Dad, you guys have supported me in everything I have done. Whether it was piano lessons, art, gymnastics, football, baseball, basketball, or ballroom dancing you guys have always been there cheering me on and that means more than you will ever know. Sabrina, my beautiful wife; you are such an inspiration to me and you have always had my back on anything I pursued. You are such an example of a godly woman and I am so thankful God has placed you in my life to strengthen me and to be my support. Mia and Maddox, thank you guys for understanding when daddy would miss those "play times" because he was working. I promise we will make them up! I love you guys more than you will ever know.

I would also like to thank my incredible faith family, CrossPointe Church. We have seen God do amazing things in our journey together and we know this is only the beginning. You guys have been such an encouragement and such an example of faith as you have consistently stepped out in faith and trusted God even when all the answers weren't there. I am so thankful for you guys. Also, to the staff, I love all of you and feel honored and humbled to serve alongside people who love the Lord as much as you do. Thank you to all of you who spent countless hours of your time reading and re-reading this material and giving your input. You guys are the best!

Thank you Janetta Oni for spending so much of your time formatting this thing and then re-formatting it! Your contribution to this material goes far beyond just formatting. You have been a faithful friend and a committed team member since my first day serving as worship pastor. I can always count on you for encouragement and for criticism. It has been a joy to see the Lord work in your life and I am excited to see the work He continues to do.

I also would like to thank Mark Steele who was the main editor on this project. You did an excellent job and were very thorough with your work. I greatly appreciate your efforts and all the time you invested in making this study more readable. Even though we have yet to officially meet in person... Thank you!

Last, but certainly not least, I want to thank Matt Herring for walking us through this whole process. You have been incredibly helpful and patient as I have texted, emailed, and called relentlessly. We could not have done this without you and I am very grateful to you, friend.

To great sections of the Church the art of worship has been lost entirely, and in its place has come that strange and foreign thing called the "program".

A.W. Tozer
The Pursuit of God

8

Foreword

Since it's beginning, Spence Parkerson has invested his life to the vision and mission of CrossPointe Church. He concerns himself not only with the spiritual life of those he leads within his ministry, but also with everyone who call CrossPointe Church their community and faith family. Spence has continued to invest his life into making disciples and centering his ministry not on the gifts that God has given him as a musician, but rather his heart for gospel centeredness and reaching people for Christ. As his pastor, it has been a privilege to serve along beside him and watch God do incredible things through him. He has a heart and passion to offer to the world not just music, but God focused understanding of worship!

The Gospel Centered Worship Leader is not just a book. It offers both a diagnoses and a cure for the issues often seen in churches where music is the root of worship instead of a redeemed and Spirit filled heart. It reveals that the culture in modern day Christianity is often unhealthy and when that spiritual vitality is missing in the hearts of its leaders it seriously undermines and diminishes the health of the entire church body. This is a book that will not only impact worship leaders everywhere, but one every church leader should read no matter what his or her focus of ministry happens to be. If you are just entering into the ministry or if you have been in ministry for a lifetime, this book will resonate with you and stir your soul as Parkerson shines the light of God's Word on your life.

-David Rogers
Lead Pastor of CrossPointe Church

10

The Back Story

I feel as though I am the least qualified to write a study on worship discipleship. I have only been leading worship for about ten years, and leading a worship ministry for about eight and I still feel as though I haven't scratched the surface on worship yet. One thing is for sure, I wasn't chosen because of my great knowledge, leadership, or abilities. I am not classically trained in music or theology. I am not well versed in all the different church structure and leadership. I am not a great public speaker or great communicator. My testimony is definitely that of God not calling the equipped, but equipping the called. But that story is for another time and place. My purpose in this book isn't to bring attention to myself or even my thoughts. It is primarily to keep worship leaders centered on Christ and give them a resource to train up and equip other worship leaders. Here is how it all started.

One day after lunch, I was walking through the church and caught a glimpse of two guys meeting in the lobby. It was obvious they were engaging in serious conversation, and recognizing them as two involved in the worship ministry, I made my way over. After a little small talk, it became clear that these two were in the middle of discipleship. The younger musician was looking to the older for training and equipping in the area of leading worship. I could sense the excitement and eagerness of the younger musician mixed with the feeling of inadequacy and anxiety of the older. After exchanging a couple more comments, I left them to start their meeting and proceeded down the hall towards my office.

Initially, I was so encouraged and excited that discipleship was happening in my ministry. Older leaders were beginning to pour into younger ones. A culture of worship and discipleship was becoming a reality in our church and in our ministry and, finally, it wasn't just me doing it! This was such a moment of joy for me… however, short lived. As pleasing and refreshing as this was to witness, the conviction began to creep in almost immediately. You see, I had been discipling and training the older musician for the past year, and I realized that he was only going to disciple the way he was discipled. Immediately I was flooded with questions of how well I had equipped him for this moment. Will he communicate what true worship is and what it isn't? Will he communicate that a worship leader must be a worshiper first? Will he communicate that we are stewards and not rock stars? Will he multiply a Christ-centered and Christ-exalting worship leader? Have *I* multiplied a Christ-centered and Christ-exalting worship leader? How have *I* trained him not just to lead on stage, but to multiply himself off stage?

The truth is that I had probably taught him about worship, but did I empower him to teach it? I probably taught him how to lead worship, but did I empower him to teach others to lead? I most likely taught him the importance of multiplying himself, but did I equip him to do it? I suddenly began to see my influence and impact outreaching me, and to be honest, it scared me. My way of training and discipling worship leaders was very organic and unstructured. I just trusted that they would learn by "seeing me in action" and our weekly meetings would serve as a spiritual check up and accountability. My main focus was training them to become biblically solid and effective worship leaders on stage. I had never thought about my impact beyond that. In that moment, I felt like I had failed him. I felt personally responsible for the outcome of this new discipleship relationship.

It was then that the Lord really impressed on me to write this study. If I was struggling with these things as a leader, how many others were? I began thinking of all the misconceptions of worship and worship leading that exists in our church culture today and the devastating effects they have on our lives as believers. Worship has become more about us than it is about God. It has become more about a song, a service, or a band than a lifestyle. It has become more about getting than giving and more selfish than selfless. We have dressed it up so much that it has become hard to tell what it is anymore. The result is a church that is dazed and confused on a battlefield in which our worship is our only hope for victory.

The Break Down

This is a 13 week study that is broken up into 3 different sections: The Worshiper, The Worship Leader, and The Good Steward.

The Worshiper: Before we begin leading others in worship, we must be worshipers first. Otherwise, we are leading people to a place that we know nothing about. The first 5 weeks of this study are devoted to laying a firm foundation of sound doctrine in the heart and mind of the worshiper. It is out of our understanding of doctrine and our experiences with God that our worship flows. We have to know what God's Word says about worship and the role of a worship leader before we stand before others and begin to do it. Allow these first several weeks to strengthen and challenge your personal life with the Lord and let His truth be the rock upon which you build your ministry.

The Worship Leader: Once we lay our foundation of doctrine, next we begin to narrow our focus to the heart of the worship leader. This section is designed to examine and expose any misconceptions or misunderstandings of what worship is and what it means to lead others. It will bring clarity to the worship leader's roles and responsibilities while bringing insight to the art of leading. Scripture will be the primary filter for this process of self-examination as we attempt to push back all of the peripheral distractions involved with leading worship and focus our attention on the heart. It is essential that the heart be the first instrument that we prepare!

The Good Steward: This final section is meant to further
condition the heart of the worship leader by focusing on the
importance of biblical leadership. Once a worshiper has been
equipped and empowered with knowledge and gifts to lead
and influence others, then they must be taught how to
appropriately use their gifts. This section is designed to do just
that. When we understand that every gift and blessing has
been given to us by God; it changes the way we use them. We
are stewards and not owners. Our positions have been
entrusted to us; we did not earn them. Hopefully, finishing the
study with this will protect the worship leader from potentially
misusing their gifts while encouraging them to continue
maximizing and multiplying them.

How To Use

This is not another book on worship, rather it is a study
guide that is meant to help create and facilitate discipleship.
The layout is very intentional and systematic; meaning, each
week builds off of the previous week; therefore, consistency in
meeting is crucial. There are discussion questions following
each week's reading that are designed to be answered
individually and discussed collectively. For example: each
person should read the selected week's reading and answer the
discussion questions individually. Then, when the weekly
group meeting takes place, the leader simply leads the group
in discussing their answers to the questions. The goal is to
create conversations and to encourage discussions in the group
and the questions are just a way to jump start that process. The
discussion questions are not meant to confine the leader or

group, rather, they are meant to serve as a spring board for conversation. Feel free to let the Spirit lead, but remember that every discussion question is there for a reason. This study will work best in groups of two or three. Any more than that could potentially take away from the intimacy and honesty that the discussion questions are trying to create.

My Prayer

My prayer is that this study will be an avenue for clarity for worship leaders today in regards to worship and stewardship. My prayer is that it will strengthen the reader's doctrine and challenge their motives. My prayer is that it will equip the reader to be a better worshiper, a better leader, and as a result, spark a desire for Gospel centered worship in our churches. My prayer is that discipleship would become a responsibility and a reality in our ministries; that we would see younger generations raised up and equipped to lead while being empowered to repeat the process. My prayer is that this study would be a catalyst to refocusing the worship of God's people back on Him. Ultimately, my prayer is to see Jesus triumphantly reigning in the hearts of worshipers while sin is continually being defeated by the power of their worship.

Section 1

The Worshiper

"We know we need to worship but we will continue to worship the wrong things. We will essentially turn into "worship zombies" who are wandering around aimlessly chasing after the thing that entices us the most."

The Worshiper

One of the most amazing truths that exists in this world today, and will continue to exist until Christ comes, is that the Gospel is advancing. This message of God's love, mercy, and judgment on His creation and the sin that corrupts it, will advance no matter what. It will advance in the face of fear. It will advance in the face of persecution. It will advance in the face of hopelessness and despair. The Gospel will continue to advance in the face of impossibility and doubt. The message of Jesus Christ will continue to advance even in the face of death. Nothing *will* stop it because nothing *can* stop it. It will continue to save souls and redeem hearts. It will continue to breathe life into dry bones. It will continue to light up even the darkest of places and it is our job, as the Church and stewards of this Gospel (1 Cor. 4:1), to see this Good News advance into and transform our communities. However, in a world corrupted by sin and riddled with distractions, this can be hard to achieve. It can be very easy to take our eyes off of Jesus and place them on other things. We *must* remain centered on the Gospel in *EVERYTHING* that we do, especially in our churches, for the Church should be the reflection of Christ to the world (Eph. 3:10).

There are many Gospel centered churches today who are passionate about seeing Christ exalted and experiencing God's presence each week. In these churches life transformation is evident and spiritual growth is a reality. There is unity and community among the believers who gather and corporate worship times are sweet and uplifting leaving the body strengthened. Every believer has an attitude of "how can I serve" instead of "how can I be served". We see diversity that reflects the community. Young and old, rich and poor, lost and found, the seekers and the servers. Racial diversity as well as social diversity is present here. The Church is the center of the community and a city on a hill. It is a place of belonging and a place of hope and refuge. All because the Gospel is present in the lives of the believers and true worship is taking place. Jesus is increasing and we are decreasing (John 3:30). However, every place of worship doesn't look like this and it is essentially a problem of worship. Everyone is worshiping something. It is unstoppable; our hearts are designed for worship. Therefore, as worship leaders, we have a job to do and that job is to keep the focus on worshiping Christ.

Broken Worship

When Jesus isn't the center of our worship then our worship becomes broken and misguided. It will suddenly turn from something that was meant to strengthen our relationship with God, to something that now hurts it. All the evidence of Christ centered worship in our lives such as peace, love, joy, strength, unity, humility, stability, and surrender will begin to fade. Slowly, we will begin to place our dependency and worth in much lesser and weaker things. Things that were never meant to carry the weight of our worship. We will begin to put our hope and trust in things that will eventually fail like health and financial security. We will search for fulfillment and satisfaction in things that are temporary like popularity, accomplishments, and relationships. We will become more and more restless as we look to those around us seeking identity and purpose. We will begin to serve and worship the cravings and desires of our flesh instead of the sufficiency of our Father. We will eventually become a slave to our own sin instead of being a slave to Christ. Without fixing our worship problem, Christ-centered worship that pleases God and draws us closer to Him will probably not be the reality in our churches. This is a scary truth because the Church's worship is preaching the loudest sermon of who God is to the world and if Jesus isn't the focus of our worship, then we have nothing to offer them.

Church could potentially turn from a place of truth, peace, and clarity to a place of deception, chaos, and confusion if Jesus isn't the center of our worship. Week after week we will continue to gather and participate in actions that are meant to draw us nearer to God as we drift further and further from Him. It may seem we are doing a lot, but there is no substance. We know we need to worship but we will continue to worship the wrong things. We will essentially turn into "worship zombies" who are wandering around aimlessly chasing after the thing that entices us the most. There is the appearance of life, but no growth. There is the appearance of God's presence, but no power. There is the appearance of community, but no love or fellowship. Our worship services should be present with the power and presence of God and should be representing His greatness to the world every single week. If our worship is misguided, our services will highlight nothing more than man's desire to belong to something greater than himself. Our times of worship will reflect more of our sin than God's holiness. We will put more emphasis on the gifts than the Giver, on the created instead of the Creator, and on our temporary enjoyment rather than His eternal worth. If we are not experiencing God's presence and seeing life transformation in our churches, then why gather? We can get everything else at our country clubs. We must continue to ask ourselves: Are we really drawing nearer to God? Is He really pleased with our services? Is lifting up Jesus our main priority? Are we really worshiping the right things? Is God's transformational power evident in the life of our churches?

We, as worship leaders, have to be aware that this could potentially be happening in our own churches and even in our own hearts. The scary part is that many believers who grew up in the church are more familiar with the traditions of the church than the character of their Father. They have more allegiance to what is known and comfortable than to what God may be doing. These churches have become self sufficient and completely satisfied without God's presence in their midst. They have substituted His presence for their traditions, His power for their entertainment, His will for their calendars, and His name for their churches'. God's work is absent while man's work is exalted.

A Church on Fire

In Acts, we see a very different church. A church that was set on fire by the power of the Holy Spirit. A church who in the midst of persecution hungered after God's word and fellowship with other believers. As a result, *"awe came upon every soul"* (Acts 2:42) and *"more than ever believers were added to the Lord, multitudes of both men and women."* (Acts 5:14) We see the disciples leaving everything behind: their jobs, their beliefs, and even their families, to follow after Jesus (Matt. 4:22). We see ordinary people, like Moses, doing extraordinary things by listening to and being obedient to God. All throughout scripture we see a great God doing great things through His people. This is what our church services should be reflecting. The dead coming alive, the lost being found, the weak made strong, the ordinary transformed into the extraordinary, and the oppressed made free, for this is the evidence of the Gospel and not merely man's traditions.

If we are going to be effective and authentic when leading people in our services, then we, as worship leaders, have to be worshipers first! We have to know where we are going. We have to know that our goal is Christ-centered worship that takes our minds off the things of this earth and puts them on God (Col.3:2). We also have to know how we are going to get there, which has everything to do with sound doctrine: our understanding of God, man, sin, and Jesus. There is no way we can worship God apart from the work of Christ (John 14:6) and the guidance of the Holy Spirit (John 14:26). Finally, we have to be familiar with God's presence and know His voice (John 10:14) so when He speaks, we can respond. How can we expect our congregations to recognize and respond to God's presence in our services if we don't? We have to start with the basics and rediscover the meaning of worship, so we can teach our congregations and get the focus back on God and off of us.

In these first several weeks, we are going to begin laying the foundation for worship and worship leading by focusing on our doctrine. We have to know where we are going before we try to lead people. We have to know how we are to get there before we take off in pursuit. We will study the doctrine of God, man, sin, and Jesus. By doing this, our doctrine will be shaped by God's word and the foundation of our worship will be firm and steady. Doctrine should not only shape and mold our worship leading, but it should drive us to worship. *"Everyone then who hears these words of mine and does them will be like a wise man who built his house on the rock. And the rain fell, and the floods came, and the winds blew and beat on that house, but it did not fall, because it had been founded on the rock." (Matt. 7:24-25)* We can't attempt to reshape our congregation's heart for worship without reshaping ours first.

By lifting up Christ and drawing near to Him during our corporate worship times, the Church will be strengthened, unified, and empowered by the Holy Spirit to impact the world. The Church doesn't need more song leaders, rather it needs more worship leaders!

Week 1

God

"We can't be satisfied with experiencing God from a distance, but we must desire to draw near to Him and see what He is like. What pleases Him? What upsets Him? Who is He? The more intimately we know God, the more intimately we worship God."

God

The only appropriate place to start on the topic of worship is God, since He is the one we are made to worship. It is important for us as worshipers to grow in knowledge and understanding of who God is in accordance to His word and His truth. We have an enemy that would like nothing more than to distort our view of God and confuse our understanding of Him and pull us away from worshiping Him (John 8:44). We can't be satisfied with experiencing God from a distance. We must desire to draw near to Him and see what He is like. What pleases Him? What upsets Him? Who is He? The more intimately we know God, the more intimately we worship God. Here is a great description of God from our church's statement of faith. Read over it a couple of times and focus on and dissect His many attributes before moving on.

There is one and only one living and true God. He is an intelligent, spiritual, and personal Being, the Creator,

Redeemer, Preserver, and Ruler of the universe. God is infinite in holiness and all other perfections. He is all powerful and all knowing; and His perfect knowledge extends to all things, past, present, and future, including the future decisions of His free creatures. To Him we owe the highest love, reverence, and obedience. The eternal triune God reveals Himself to us as Father, Son, and Holy Spirit, with distinct personal attributes, but without division of nature, essence, or being.[15]

As you see, there is so much depth to our God that our natural minds cannot comprehend all that He is. This is why we need His Spirit to reveal it to us (1 Cor. 2:9-10). We will dive deeper into some of these attributes now and cover some of the others later.

God is Life

"For from Him and through Him and to Him are all things. To Him be glory forever. Amen." Romans 11:36

In other words, all things find their being, their meaning, and their purpose in God. There is nothing that has ever existed or will ever exist, seen or unseen, apart from Him and His purpose. John 5:26 says that *"the Father has life in Himself"* meaning that He doesn't rely on anything to sustain Him, but Himself. He doesn't need oxygen, food, or water to keep Him alive like we do. We *have* life. He *is* life. He is complete. He lacks nothing and depends on nothing (Acts 17:25). Therefore, nothing can give Him life, rather since He is life, He gives life to all things. He was never made or created, He simply always was and He always will be (Rev.

1:8). This truth is best revealed in Gen. 1:1, *"in the beginning"*, before anything had life, meaning, or purpose... God was there seeing the possibilities. And with just a spoken word, He creates life and existence. He is the Creator and all of His creation exists for Him and to reflect His glory (Psalm 19:1).

God is Spirit

"To the King of ages, immortal, invisible, the only God, be honor and glory forever and ever. Amen." 1 Timothy 1:17

God is everywhere always! He reigns over all... at all times. Nothing is outside His knowledge, His reach, His understanding, His power, His presence, or His control. Nothing can escape God because He is everywhere (Ps. 139:7-12). He is not confined to any geographical location therefore, there is no place that He cannot be found. He is not limited by time. He is just as much God today as He was yesterday and will be tomorrow. Time *does not* and *cannot* contain Him. He is eternal (Ps. 90: 1-4, Ps. 139:16). God is omnipresent. He is not limited by any physical matter or attributes that we humans are confined to, such as our frail and failing bodies, our limited senses, and our limited ability to understand and comprehend. We see in John 4:24 that *"God is spirit"* and Jesus says in Luke 24:39, referring to His resurrected body, that *"a spirit does not have flesh and bones"*. God does not have a physical body that limits Him in any way. He is everywhere, always, and He never tires or grows weary (Jer. 40:28). God also is omniscient. He knows everything (1 John 3:20). There is nothing that catches Him by

surprise or impresses Him in any way. He knows our thoughts
and our movements before we think them and do them (Ps.
139: 1-4). He never has questions or wonders about anything.
He has all the understanding and all the answers all of the
time!

God is Holy

*"Exalt the Lord our God, and worship at his holy mountain;
for the Lord our God is holy!" Psalm 99:9*

God is completely and absolutely perfect. There isn't
anything in Him that is evil or wrong in any way. He doesn't
have issues or struggles like we do. He is not like us. He has
never been or will ever be tempted to sin (James 1:13). He is
morally spotless in character and action, upright, pure, and
untainted with evil desires, motives, thoughts, words, or acts.[1]
Not only is God completely free from any and everything
wicked, wrong, or sinful, He can't even look upon sin or be
near it (Hab. 1:13). We see this play out in the Garden when
Adam and Eve sin; they are then banned from God's presence
(Gen. 3:23-24). God's holiness not only describes who He is,
but also where He is, like His dwelling place (Ps. 24:3-4) and
His presence (Ex. 26:33). When God spoke to Moses, the
place where he was standing became holy (Ex. 3:5) and when
God comes down to Mount Sinai, Moses has to set boundaries
around the mountain so no one will touch it (Ex.19:12). His
holiness demands respect, reverence, and fear from all of His
creation (Ps. 33:8, Luke 1:50).

God is Just

"The Rock, his work is perfect, for all his ways are justice. A God of faithfulness and without iniquity, just and upright is he." Deuteronomy 32:4

God is just. Everything He does is right and fair (Isaiah 61:8). There is no unbalance in Him (2 Chronicles 19:7). His actions are in perfect alignment with His character. He is always observing and nothing is hidden from His sight and everything must one day give an account to Him (Prov. 15:3, Hebrews 4:13). Evil will be punished and righteousness and obedience to Him will be rewarded (Prov. 11:21, Romans 6:23). God's justice demands that wrongs committed against Him be paid for and reconciled. God's wrath is His way of executing His justice to those who refuse to follow Him. God's wrath protects His holiness. We stated earlier that God is holy and completely free from sin. God's wrath is what is being stored up (Romans 2:5) and will one day be poured out upon all sin and unrighteousness (Romans 1:18), finally settling the score and making all things right with Him again. One misconception could be that God's justice works against His love or vice versa. This is not the case. His love and justice work together and the greatest example of this is seen in Christ and His work on the Cross. God's justice requires that there be payment of the penalty of sin, while God's love desires humans to be restored to fellowship with Him.[2]

God is Good

"Oh, how abundant is your goodness, which you have stored up for those who fear you and worked for those who take refuge in you, in the sight of the children of mankind!" Psalm 31:19

God's goodness can't really be confined to or contained by a definition. It can be seen, heard, and felt, but it is difficult to define it as one thing. This is because God's goodness is the summation of everything that He is, does, and feels. It approves when He is pleased (Gen. 1:31). It disapproves when He is grieved (Gen. 6: 5-7). It motivates Him to act or not to act. It causes Him to give or not to give, to bless or not to bless. Just as we discussed in the last section, God's holiness separates Himself from us. However, it's His goodness that draws us near to Him (Romans 5:8-9). His goodness manifests itself throughout scripture by His love (John 3:16, 1 John 4:9-12) and His desire for all humanity to be reconciled to Him. Also, His goodness reveals itself through His grace (Eph. 2:8-9), His mercy (Deut. 4:31), His righteousness (Jer. 9:23-24), His kindness/forbearance/patience (Romans 2:4), His faithfulness (Ps. 33:4, 2 Tim. 2:13), His sovereignty (Proverbs 16:4), and even His discipline (Proverbs 3:12). For the believer, God's goodness is the ultimate source of peace, for we know that He is working all things out for His good (Romans 8:28).

Discussion

A) Discuss any moments of challenge, conviction, or encouragement during this week's reading.

B) What is your purpose on this earth? Is it to be the smartest in your class, the best on your team, or the most respected in your circle of friends? Maybe it's to be financially stable and secure or to be the best parent for your kids? Read Romans 11:36 and discuss how this impacts your outlook on your life. How does this impact your worship?

C) When we think about worship, we typically think of singing songs and any other act that we do in our services at church. How does knowing that God is spirit challenge that mindset? If God isn't confined to time or space then what is Romans 12:1 saying about our worship of Him?

D) Read this quote by R.C. Sproul and read Isaiah 6:1-5 and discuss how a deeper understanding of God's holiness changes our view of God, ourselves, and how we respond to Him.
"When we understand the character of God, when we grasp something of His holiness, then we begin to understand the radical character of our sin and hopelessness."[3]

E) When hard times come, do you worry or do you worship? In times of uncertainty, do you stress or do you trust? If God is good and everything He does is good, how does that change the way we face trials and times of uncertainty? Read Jeremiah 29: 11 and Romans 8:28 and discuss the way believing and trusting in God's goodness impacts your worship.

F) Discuss some other attributes of God and how they deepen your worship of Him.

Take Away: Our worship is a direct representation of our understanding of God!

Week 2

Man

"We have a specific purpose and reason for being created and that purpose is to worship God."

Man

In the last section, we discovered that the more we know God and learn about Him, the deeper and more mature our worship of Him will be and therefore, the more pleasing our worship will be to Him. In the same way, learning about who we are is essential to growing and maturing as a worshiper because it affects the way we view God. Having a solid doctrine of man is only going to strengthen our doctrine of God. He is our Creator and the attributes and characteristics of the Creator can be seen in His creation. We have a specific purpose and reason for being created and that purpose is to worship God. At one time in history, this purpose was all that we knew and it was all that mattered to us. In the beginning, we existed in harmony with our Creator and were fulfilling our created purpose. However, sin entered the picture and has now distorted, confused, and created separation where there was only meant to be peace, clarity, and unity between God and man. As stated in the last section, God's holiness will not allow Him to be associated with anything unholy or imperfect, which is sin. We will dive deeper in to sin in the next section, but for now we will focus on who man is and why we were created.

Who Are We

"Then God said, "Let us make man in our image, after our likeness. And let them have dominion over the fish of the sea and over the birds of the heavens and over the livestock and over all the earth and over every creeping thing that creeps on the earth." So God created man in his own image, in the image of God he created him; male and female he created them." Genesis 1:26-27

Man is the special creation of God, made in His own image. We were created by Him and for Him (Psalm 100:3). From the very beginning of scripture we see that before anything existed or was, God was there (Gen. 1:1-3). Man was created on the sixth day of creation and upon creating him the Creator gave His approval by stating that His creation was "very good" (Gen. 1:31). He was formed of the dust of the earth and was endowed with soul life by the breath of God. God is the source of his life, and dust the material of his being[4]. By this we see that man is more precious in God's sight than all other creation (Matt. 10:31, Matt. 12:12) as he was "breathed" upon by the eternal life-giving breath of the Creator giving man a soul (Gen. 2:7) thus, man now bearing the image of his Creator. However, we also see that by being formed from the dust of the earth, man is inferior and subordinate to his Creator reminding us that even though we are created "in His image", we are not equal with Him (Psalm 8:3-6). Being a created being, we look to God for our purpose and our provision just like all of creation. We are not satisfied or fulfilled apart from Him (Psalm 104: 27-30). Being "in His image", we are different from the rest of creation in that we are capable of having a conscious personal relationship with the Creator and of responding to him, can know God and understand what he desires [of us], can love, worship, and obey [our] Maker[5]. A.W. Tozer says it best, *"Being made in His image we have within us the capacity to know Him. In our sins we lack only the power. The moment the Spirit has quickened us to life in regeneration our whole being senses it's kinship to God and leaps up in joyous recognition."* [6]

What Is Our Purpose

"Oh come, let us worship and bow down; let us kneel before the Lord, our Maker! For He is our God, and we are the people of his pasture, and the sheep of his hand." -Psalm 95:6-7

Creation has no other purpose than to point to the magnificence of its Creator. In Psalm 19 we see that the *"heavens declare the glory of God and the sky above proclaims His handiwork."* Everything God creates, He creates because He has a specific purpose for it. That purpose is to worship Him and bring Him glory! The definition for glory is "high renown or honor won by notable achievements." Just like an accomplished athlete has many different awards and trophies that exist for no other reason than to bring attention to their accomplishments, everything created, exists primarily to bring recognition and attention to the Creator. The heavens reveal the uncontained and unimagined greatness of God. The skies reveal His majesty and splendor. The oceans reveal the depth of His power and might (Psalm 93:4). The mountains reveal His faithfulness and great strength and in man, we see God's limitless love and grace (Romans 5:8). According to the Westminster Shorter Catechism, man's chief end is to "glorify God and to enjoy Him forever." We exist for no other reason than to worship Him and find our greatest sense of satisfaction, purpose, and fulfillment in Him. Nothing takes priority over this purpose and nothing can ever be more important for our existence (1 Cor. 10:31). Three ways that we glorify God are through relationship, reflection, and growth.

Relationship

"And this is eternal life, that they know you the only true God, and Jesus Christ whom you have sent." John 17:3

When Jesus was questioned as to what the greatest commandment was, His response was, *"You shall love the Lord your God with all your heart and with all your soul and with all your mind" (Matt. 22:37).* Jesus is telling us that an intimate personal relationship with God is the most important thing we could ever attain in this life. In fact, it's what God desires. We see intimate fellowship with God and Adam and Eve in the Garden before the Fall (Gen. 3:8-9). I can only imagine all God communicated to Adam about Himself; His thoughts, His plans, and His power, while they "walked together" in the "cool of the day." We see, more so in man than all other creation, God's desire to be known… not just in part, but in whole. God doesn't NEED us to know Him; He wants us to because He delights in His people (Ps. 149:4). He desires to be known and to dwell with and among His people (Ex. 29:45-46). For God, being known means being glorified because upon truly knowing Him, "tasting and seeing that He is good" (Psalm 34:8), there is no other response (Ex. 34:6-8). We are promised that if we draw near to God, then He will draw near to us (James 4:8). The more we fellowship with God, the more we know Him. The more we know Him, the more we worship Him. And the more we worship Him, the more we glorify Him.

Reflection

"Therefore, we are ambassadors for Christ, God making His appeal through us." 2 Corinthians 5:20

We stated earlier that the greatest commandment is to *"love the Lord your God with all your heart, soul, and mind,"* according to Matthew 22:37. However, Jesus goes on to say that the second greatest commandment is to *"love your neighbor as yourself"* (Matt. 22:39). These two commandments are speaking of a vertical, personal relationship with God as well as a horizontal relationship with each other. In other words, God is not only glorified when we know Him, but also when we accurately reflect Him to each other. We are His representatives. We are His workmanship, created for good works (Eph. 2:10) so that all may see Him in us. Jesus says it best in John 14:9 when he says, *"Whoever has seen me has seen the Father also."* Just like a mirror reflects the object that is looking into it, we are to be a reflection to the world of God, our Creator. Another way to view it is that our lives are living sermons to all those around us as to who God is and what He is like. Much like Paul in Acts 9:15, we are chosen instruments for God to carry His name to all those around us and into all the world. We can't accurately reflect Him if we don't know Him. We must rely on His spirit, His strength, and His love to control us as we share Him and reflect Him to the world (2 Cor. 5:14-15).

Growth

"so as to walk in a manner worthy of the Lord, fully pleasing to Him, bearing fruit in every good work and increasing in the knowledge of God." Colossians 1:10

Growth is the evidence of life and God is life so, where God is present, growth is inevitable. God is glorified not only in our relationship to Him and our reflection of Him to others, but also in our growth. His desire is for Himself and His character to increase in our lives while our sinfulness and brokenness decreases (John 3:30) through the power of His Spirit at work within us. He is continually shaping and molding us, through our experiences and even our failures, more and more into His image (Phil. 1:6). Just like a potter starts with a lump of clay and shapes and molds it into a beautiful piece of pottery, the Lord is shaping us as well (Isaiah 64:8). God uses many different things to grow us in our relationship with Him. He gives us His word to teach us about Himself and what He expects from us (Hebrews 4:12). He also gives us His Spirit that challenges, convicts, and leads us into His truth (John 16:13). God also uses circumstances and even

trials in our lives to refine and strengthen our faith in Him
(James 1:2-4). The more we grow in Him and His ways, the
more His nature and image are evident in our lives as
believers. The more God sees Himself in us, the more He is
glorified. John Piper says it best when he says, *"God is most
glorified in us when we are most satisfied in Him."* [16]

Discussion

A) Discuss any moments of challenge, conviction, or encouragement during this week's reading.

B) Read Romans 1:21-23. Although they knew about God in their minds, that knowledge and understanding had not transformed their hearts into worshiping Him and honoring Him as God. We have the same problem today. Many people believe they are Christians because they acknowledge God, but their lives are not reflecting in worship of Him. It is not enough to simply know about God or know Him from a distance. He desires intimacy and wants to be Lord of our lives. Discuss the differences between having an intimate relationship with the Lord and just knowing about Him.

C) Now read John 17:3 and John 17:26. In verse 3 Jesus states that the sole purpose of life is for us to "know God" and in verse 26 He recalls that in His ministry and life He served as a great reflection for God. We know from Hebrews 1:3 that Jesus is the "*radiance of the glory of God and the exact imprint of his nature.*" If your life was a mirror, what would it reflect? Your desires or His desires? Your will or His? Your sinfulness or His holiness?

D) I have often heard it said: "*If you are not growing, you are dying.*" As believers, growth is not an option; it must be taking place or we begin to drift. I love Perry

Noble's quote on drifting. He says, "*No one drifts closer to God! Focused people are driven towards God. Unfocused drifters are lazy and drift towards sin!*" [17] Read Psalm 1:1-4 and talk about areas in your life that you could be more disciplined and focused on growing in your relationship with God.

Take Away: Man's purpose is to know God, to enjoy God, and to worship God forever!

Week 3

"Where God is holy, sin is filthy. Where God is pure, sin is perverted. Where God brings truth, sin brings deception. Where God brings life, sin brings death and destruction."

Sin

So far, we have looked at who God is and who man is. Now we are going to introduce the great chasm that stands between them both … Sin. We know God is holy, righteous, and good in all His ways. Man, being His creation, is meant to bring God pleasure by worshiping Him and reflecting Him to others. Sin disrupts this purpose and causes distance between God and man where there was meant to be nearness. It causes conflict where there was meant to be peace. Sin causes rebellion where there was meant to be obedience and separation where there was meant to be fellowship. Simply put, sin is a state of alienation from God[7]. It is the outright rejection and independence from God's will and purpose. It desires to rob God of His glory and challenge His rule. Where God is holy, sin is filthy. Where God is pure, sin is perverted. Where God brings truth, sin brings deception. Where God brings life, sin brings death and destruction. As man, we find ourselves not only caught in the middle of this struggle, but *"dead in our sin and trespasses" (Eph. 2:1).* We are helpless and hopeless in our state and that is why Jesus is so important! We will talk about Him and His work in the next section. For now, we will focus on sin.

Definition of Sin

1) *Hamartema* – this word translated in the Greek means "to miss a mark" much like an archer missing the bull's eye on his target. This definition really speaks of man's inability to live up to God's standard and puts the focus and the attention on God's holiness and His otherness (Hab. 1:13). A great example of this is Moses, upon encountering the Lord in Exodus 3:5-6, keeping his distance, removing his sandals, and hiding his face. Moses was afraid to look at God because of his own unworthiness and sin in the presence of such holiness. As worshipers, the more we know and experience God's holiness, the more aware we are of our sinfulness and depravity.

2) *Parabasis* – this word translated in the Greek means "to overstep a forbidden line" much like someone who trespasses on property that is not their own or crosses over an area specifically marked off, such as a crime scene. This definition points to our active part and responsibility in finding ourselves in this state. In Genesis 3:16-17, God lays out the boundaries for man to *"eat of every tree in the garden, but of the tree of the knowledge of good and evil you shall not eat for in the day that you eat of it you shall surely die."* Just a couple passages later, we see the transgression of Man; the conscious decision to disobey and rebel from the

boundaries that God had set in place. We, as mankind, are not just innocent victims when it comes to sin. We are all guilty of actively rebelling against God (Isaiah 53:5, Romans 3:10-12).

The Origin of Sin

It is important for us to understand the origin of sin as we prepare to fight it. A common understanding for many believers is that sin originated, or started, when Adam and Eve chose to disobey God and rebel against Him. This is where sin corrupts mankind, however, this is not where sin starts. Sin existed before the fall of man in the heart of Lucifer when he chose to challenge God and attempt to steal His worship. Sin isn't an "oops" moment when Adam and Eve messed up; it is the weapon of the great enemy of God and when we don't see it this way, we run the risk of diluting the gravity of it and weakening it's power in our minds and hearts.

Before Adam and Eve in the Garden. Before Cain murders Abel. Before Sodom and Gomorrah…sin existed. Sin existed in the universe before it existed on the earth. Evidence of this is found in the Garden when the serpent, with sin already controlling him, deceives Adam and Eve into sinning against God (Gen. 3:1-5). Sin originated with Lucifer, or Satan (1 John 3:8), one of God's angels, as he desired equality with God and chose to rebel and actively seek to rob God of His glory (Isaiah 14:12-15). This act of defiance and mutiny results in Satan being cast out of God's presence, along with his angels, and ultimately being defeated forever by the sinless blood of Jesus and His glorious resurrection (Rev. 12:7-11). While this treachery proved unsuccessful, it did, nevertheless, introduce into the universe a new evil element hitherto unknown. The perverted principle was sin. Lucifer degenerated into the devil and became, therefore, the source and strength of sin. [8]

While an angel introduced sin into the universe, it was a man who invited it into the world [9] (Gen. 3). Now, this same sin that caused one of God's angels to rebel against Him now lurks within us… all of us (Romans 5:12). It is important for us, as worshipers, to grasp this because many of us view sin as a minor inconvenience that we sometimes struggle with instead of seeing it as the major weapon that God's enemy, Satan, is using against Him and His children. There is an enemy and his desire is the destruction and devastation of God's will and plan (John 10:10) and we, as worshipers, are on the front lines.

Now that we have an understanding of where sin comes from, we can look at how it has infected and affected human nature ever since the Fall. Here are some characteristics of the effects of sin in and on mankind.

Sin Separates

"…but your iniquities have made a separation between you and your God, and your sins have hidden his face from you so that he does not hear." Isaiah 59:2

Before Adam and Eve encountered the serpent in the Garden, they enjoyed fellowship with God. However, upon making the conscious decision to go against God's purpose and rebel against His lordship over their lives, this is the moment when sin infects human nature (Romans 5:12). Now, all of mankind finds itself in a state of separation from God.

Through Adam's transgression, he invited sin into human nature and now every human is born into sin and cut off from God's presence. This is the "death" that God is referring to in Gen. 2:17, not a physical death but more, a spiritual death… separation from Him. This separation is suffered by ALL (Romans 3:23, 3:10-12) regardless of our good deeds or works. We are dead in our sin and cut off from God's presence with no way of changing our condition, much like a dead man has no power to *not* be dead. However, the beauty of the Gospel is that while we were dead in our sin, Jesus came and rescued us by going to the cross and canceling our debt. Through His resurrection, He defeated sin and death and restored us back to peace and fellowship with God (Romans 5:8, Colossians 2:13-15, Romans 6:23). This is called *justification* and it is only applied to the believer (Romans 5:1, John 14:6).

Sin Deteriorates

"But I say, walk by the Spirit, and you will not gratify the desires of the flesh. For the desires of the flesh are against the Spirit, and the desires of the Spirit are against the flesh, for these are opposed to each other, to keep you from doing the things you want to do." Galatians 5:16-17

Once the believer has been raised with Christ as a new creation (2 Cor. 5:17), the penalty of sin, which is death, is erased. However, the effects of sin remain because we are still in the flesh. Our eternal position of reconciliation with God is secure, but our temporary state, is still affected. Immediately our sin nature goes to war with God's Spirit dwelling in us and the tug of war begins. God's Spirit begins the process of *sanctification*: shaping and molding the believer more and more into His perfect image by urging and empowering the believer to rid himself of the effects of his sin (Philippians 1:6, Colossians 3:1-10, John 16:13). Sanctification is a process of God's Spirit moving the believer toward Him, while the believer's sin nature is pulling him away from God. Even Paul himself speaks of personally facing this struggle in Romans 7:16-20. It is our responsibility to "put to death" what is earthly in us (Col. 3:5), such as pride, selfishness, lust, greed, impurity, etc. and put on the new self, which is hidden in Christ. We must decide to walk in the Spirit while putting our sin to death everyday. If left alone, sin will deteriorate the faith of the believer and weaken his strength to resist it (Hebrews 3:13). This is why it is so important for the believer to "cast off" and "get rid" of the sin that so easily entangles us and fix our eyes on Jesus, the Author and the Perfecter of our faith (Heb. 12: 1-2).

Sin Eliminates

"The thief comes only to steal and kill and destroy. I came that they may have life and have it abundantly." John 10:10

Sin is never satisfied. It's goal and ultimate end is death and destruction (Romans 6:23) and it does not relent until it destroys. We see throughout scripture that sin is crouching, waiting, and roaming around seeking and desiring someone to devour (Gen. 4:7, 1 Peter 5:8). The final destination of sin is not a pleasant place. It is a place of fiery torment and pain where there is much suffering (Matt. 13:41-42) and the suffering and punishment never ends (Matt. 25:46). However, though sin may be strong and have influence over our flesh (Matt. 26:41), God has conquered sin and death once and for all through Jesus Christ (1 Cor. 15:57) and those who are found in Him are eternally secure through the Holy Spirit for the day of redemption (Eph. 4:30). There is nothing that can condemn the justified (Romans 8:1), undo what Christ has already accomplished (Col. 1:13-14), or snatch us away from the grip of a God whose power is greater and whose love goes further than anything in existence (Romans 8:38-39). Praise be to God!

Discussion

A) Discuss any moments of challenge, conviction, or encouragement during this week's reading.

B) By linking the origin of sin back to Lucifer, or Satan, we have the opportunity not only to see where sin started, but also where it leads. Now Satan is eternally cast out of the presence of God and will one day be thrown into eternal fire (Rev. 20:10) because of his rebellion towards God. Many Christians and non-Christians today view sin as a minor imperfection that God is unhappy with, but tolerates. How does making this connection with sin and Satan deepen your understanding of sin and change your attitude toward sin in your life?

C) Read 2 Timothy 3:1-5 and observe how many of these characteristics that you identify in your own life.

D) One of the effects of sin on the human heart is a hardening toward the things of God: truth, holiness, righteousness, peace, selflessness, humility, etc. (Matt. 13:15). As we stated earlier, sin deteriorates the believer's desire to please God and ignites the desire to please self. Read Ephesians 6:10-18 and evaluate your pursuit of holiness and godliness in your own walk with Christ. Are you "being strong in the Lord" and standing firm against the "schemes of the devil"? Discuss practical ways you can defend yourself from the attacks of the enemy everyday by remembering the tools that God has given us to overcome sin in our daily life. God's word, Jesus, the Holy Spirit, fellowship of believers, and prayer are all the power we need to live lives free from the bondage of sin.

E) As worship leaders, we have a responsibility to teach our congregations about the severity of sin in our lives; however, we do not want to give sin any more attention than it deserves. The truth is, we have a Savior who has given His life for our ransom and now His victory is ours! So we want to make sure we are exalting Jesus as we lead and not sin. Discuss the importance of finding a healthy balance of communicating the severity of sin without it overshadowing the power of Christ to our congregations each week.

Take Away: Sin is man's sickness and Jesus is the only cure!

Week 4

"It is because of Him
that we, who were
once far off, can now
be brought near to
the Lord and know
and enjoy fellowship
with Him again."

Jesus

Jesus Christ is the answer! He is the answer to our sin problem and to solving our state of separation from God. Sin's grip on the individual is loosed by the work of Christ: *"through Christ Jesus the law of the Spirit of life set me free from the law of sin and death"* (Rom. 8:2).[10] It is by and through Him, and only Him, that we are redeemed and restored to the Father (John 14:6) and our sins are washed away (1 John 1:7). He accomplished this by coming to earth and dying as a perfect sacrifice (1 Peter 1:19) for our sins to appease God's wrath for our rebellion. His perfect blood was the only adequate payment for our debt. Anything else would have been insufficient. Man has nothing of worth to bring to a Holy God. A divine sacrifice is the only payment to settle a wrong inflicted upon a divine God. Jesus bridges this gap and settles this debt for us! It is because of Him that we, who were once far off, can now be brought near to the Lord and know and enjoy fellowship with Him again (Eph. 2:13). In light of our depravity, that is our "moral corruption", He is our hope (1 Tim. 1:1). In light of our desperation, He is our salvation (Titus 2:11-14, Hebrews 9:27-28, John 3:16). In man's current state of enmity with God, Jesus brings peace and reconciliation (Romans 5:1). In regards to our faith, He is not only the author of it, but He is the perfecter as well (Hebrews 12:2). He has done everything for us and He should mean everything to the worshiper; for without Him, worshiping God is impossible.

Now that we have a good understanding of what Jesus accomplished through His ministry on the earth, we will now focus our attention on how He accomplished it. There are a couple of essential doctrines and understandings about Jesus that all believers must accept. I will try to cover them all here as we look at His birth, His life, His death, and His resurrection.

His Birth

"And the Word became flesh and dwelt among us, and we have seen his glory, glory as of the only Son from the Father, full of grace and truth." John 1:14

If part of Jesus' role was to satisfy God's wrath against our trespass and be an adequate substitute and representation for us, there is one doctrine that we must understand. The *hypostatic union* is the coming together of two distinct natures, deity and humanity, in the person of Jesus Christ. These two natures dwelled completely in Christ at the same time. If we said anything else, we would be contradicting prophecy, scripture, and even Jesus Himself for He said, *"I*

and the Father are one" (John 10:30) and *"anyone who has
seen me has seen the Father"* (John 14:9) and Colossians 2:9
says, *"For in him the whole fullness of deity dwells bodily."*

Jesus' divinity qualifies His death in the eyes of God
because even though He was a man, He was still holy and
acceptable in God's sight because He was divine. Hebrews 1:3
says, *"He is the radiance of the glory of God and the exact
imprint of his nature."* The death of Christ is sufficient for all
sinners who have ever lived, for it was not merely a finite
human, but an infinite God who died. He, the Life, the Giver
and Sustainer of life, who did not have to die, died.[11] Jesus'
humanity brings God near and shows us His character
allowing Jesus to be our perfect example of humanity, the way
God designed in the beginning. Jesus' humanity also qualifies
His offering a sacrifice, His life, on our behalf because He was
one of us and could identify with us in every way (Heb.
4:14-15).

The virgin birth of Jesus is so important because it is where
these two distinct natures join together.

His Life

*"who, though he was in the form of God, did not count
equality with God a thing to be grasped, but made himself
nothing, taking the form of a servant, being born in the
likeness of men. And being found in human form, he humbled
himself by becoming obedient to the point of death, even death
on a cross." Philippians 2:6-8*

Jesus' birth focuses our attention on His two complete and
distinct natures, humanity and divinity, coming together in His

being. However, as Jesus grew and His ministry began, we see Him as the perfect revelation of God in flesh (Col. 1:19) to humanity. Not only did Jesus teach us about who God is, He showed us by the way He lived. We see God's power revealed through Jesus in many ways. Jesus performed miracles like turning water into wine (John 2:1-11), feeding the five thousand (Matt. 14:13-21), and the transfiguration (Matt. 17:1-13). He also performed healings like raising Lazarus from the dead (John 11:38-44) and healing the paralytic (Luke 5:17-26). He also performed many wonders such as calming the storm (Matt. 8:23-27) and walking on water (Matt. 14:22-27).

Being fully God, it is easy for us to see how Jesus accomplished all of these acts; but Jesus was also fully man. This concept racks our brains and challenges our understanding a bit. Being human, Jesus experienced all the limitations of human nature physically, mentally, and spiritually; but yet performed these great miracles and wonders while remaining sinless. An understanding of *The Trinity* is crucial to explaining how Jesus accomplished all that He was sent to accomplish while being confined in human form. The Trinity simply put is the threefold manifestation of the one God as Father, Son, and Holy Spirit.[12] This relationship is best described in this way in regards to our salvation: The Father planned it, the Son purchased it, and the Holy Spirit applies it to us.[13] The first evidence of all three persons of the Godhead revealing themselves simultaneously during Jesus' ministry was at His baptism (Matt. 3:13-17). Jesus was completely reliant on His Father for everything (John 5:19) and completely filled with the Holy Spirit (Luke 4:1) to fulfill His task while the Father and the Holy Spirit

were reliant on the Son to carry out the Father's plan. The idea
that three distinct persons could exist in one completely goes
beyond our ability to rationalize as humans. Therefore the
Trinity is a matter of faith for the believer maybe more so than
other doctrines. This quote by Augustine sums up the doctrine
of the Trinity for the believer. *Try to explain it, and you'll lose
your mind; but try to deny it, and you'll lose your soul.*

His Death

*"For our sake he made him to be sin who knew no sin, so that
in him we might become the righteousness of God." 2
Corinthians 5:21*

In the Old Testament, before Jesus enters the scene, there is
a very complex system set up by God for His people to make
atonement for their sins. As we discussed earlier, God is holy,
righteous, pure in every way, and free from sin. As we also
discussed, we are not. Our sin separates us from God and
places us under His judgment and therefore, God's people
needed a way to appease God's wrath. Every year the High
Priest would offer up two goats as atonement for the sins of
the people. One goat would be slain (Lev. 16:15) to satisfy the
wrong committed against God. The other goat would have all
the sins of the people imputed, or transferred, to it as the High
Priest laid his hands on its head and sent it away into the
wilderness (Lev. 16:21-22) symbolizing a removal of sin from
the people. However, this process only accomplished in part
what Jesus was to accomplish in whole.

The first goat represents Jesus in that His perfect blood
satisfies the penalty of our offense to God and His wrath is

appeased (Romans 3:23-25), and through the shedding of His blood we can be forgiven (Heb. 9:22). The second goat represents Jesus in that all of man's sin was imputed to Jesus and He who knew no sin, then became sin on our behalf. Just as the goat removes sin from the people, Jesus removes sin from His people (John 1:29).

There is one more player in this scenario that points to Jesus and that is the High Priest. Much like the high priest of the Old Testament served as a representative from God to the people and a representative of the people to God, Jesus does the same for us (Heb. 4:14-15). He continues to stand in the gap for us (1 Tim. 2:5).

His Resurrection

"And if Christ has not been raised, your faith is futile and you are still in your sins." 1 Corinthians 15:17

Why is the resurrection important if Jesus' death was sufficient to satisfy God's wrath against our sin? If Jesus' sinless blood was enough to forgive us of our sin then why do we need the resurrection?

The resurrection of Jesus is everything to the believer, for without it, Jesus was not who He said He was and did not accomplish what He said He would. Along with many prophecies made about the coming Christ (Isaiah 53:5-6, Jer. 23:5, Micah 5:2), Jesus Himself made many assertions about His divinity and His purpose to save His people from their sins. To name a few, Jesus stated that He was the *"light of the world"* (John 8:12), that He was *"from above and not of this world"* (John 8:23). In John 10:28 He says, *"I give them eternal life, and they will never perish, and no one will snatch them out of my hand."* Finally, Jesus specifically says that He is the *"resurrection and the life"* and that everyone who *"lives and believes in me shall never die"* in John 11:25-26. Probably one of the most famous is found in John 14:6 where Jesus states, *"I am the way, and the truth, and the life. No one comes to the Father except through me."*

All of these declarations are a source of hope for the believer and inspire faith that salvation is possible through Jesus and reconciliation with the Father is a reality. However, without the resurrection, there is no hope and no reason for faith for we are still trapped in our sin because Jesus would not have overcome it. For we know that the penalty of our sin is death (Romans 6:23) and where there is no resurrection, death still reigns. As long as death reigns, God's people are still trapped in their sin and separated from Him, but praise God that death has been defeated!

The resurrection of Jesus Christ is God showing His acceptance and approval of Jesus' work of redeeming mankind and atoning for their sin (Romans 4:25). It is God confirming with a loud shout that Jesus is who He said He was and He did what He said He would do. Now we have confidence and faith that Jesus is alive forevermore and that He holds the keys to Death and Hades (Rev. 1:17-18). Death has been swallowed up in His victory and can no longer have a hold on those who are in Christ and covered by His blood (1 Cor. 15:54-56, Col. 2:12-13). Now that Jesus has been vindicated and validated by the Father through His resurrection, we can know that there is nothing that can separate us from the love of the Father (Romans 8:37-39).

Discussion

A) Discuss any moments of challenge, conviction, or encouragement during this week's reading.

B) Throughout this section we have talked about who Jesus is and what He accomplished on our behalf during His ministry on this earth. Now the question is to whom does this apply and how? Jesus says in John 14:6, *"I am the way, and the truth, and the life. No one comes to the Father except through me."* Jesus' blood and atonement are only applied to those who have been buried with Him (Col. 2:12) and raised with Him (Col. 3:1). These verses are describing a death and a resurrection for those who have been united with Christ. In other words, not everyone will be saved and forgiven of their sins. Only those who trust Jesus as their Savior and Lord and follow Him with all that they are. How does this message go against many of the prosperity gospel and universalists' messages that are so popular in our culture today?

C) Read Matthew 16:24-25.
How do we see this passage played out in the life of the disciples? How did they deny themselves? What did they leave behind (Matt. 4:20-22, 9:9)?
How has this passage been played out in your life? What have you left behind to follow Christ? In what ways are you a new creation (2 Cor. 5:17)?

D) As a believer, you have benefited from the obedience of the disciples to "go and make disciples" as Jesus commanded them to in Matt. 28:19. You have heard and had a chance to respond to the Gospel because of their faithfulness. In what ways are you being faithful to this command knowing that not all will be saved?

E) In Matthew 6, Jesus is speaking to religious people who put their spirituality and good deeds on display for others to see and be impressed. We know that God is more concerned with our heart to please Him (Psalm 24:3-4) than our works to please others. As worshipers, and even worship leaders, is the majority of our spiritual life on display for others? Are our prayers more passionate when others are listening? Is our worship more intense when we have on-lookers? If so, who are we worshiping?

F) One of the most frightening passages is found in Matthew 7:21 when Jesus says, *"Not everyone who says to me, 'Lord, Lord,' will enter the kingdom of heaven."* This speaks of an absence of unity with Christ and a presence of disillusionment caused by sin. It goes on to say *"did we not prophesy in your name and cast out demons in your name."* As worship leaders, we can substitute these words with, *"Did we not sing songs about you and for you? Did we not even write songs for you?"*
Read Matthew 7:21 again, the whole verse. What is the will of God? Read 1 Thessalonians 4:3. Discuss how our priorities privately and publicly as worship leaders should change knowing that God is concerned with the

sanctification of our congregations and not just the energy and charisma of our services.

Take Away: In Jesus; our trespass of sin has been reconciled, our purpose restored, and our worship revived!

Week 5

the Compartmentalization conflict

"Worship sanctifies the believer and evangelizes to the unbeliever."

The Compartmentalization Conflict

Before we move on to the next section, I want to introduce one more thing that should help us visualize everything we have been talking about up to this point. In short, we have discussed that man exists for the sole purpose of giving glory to God, his creator. However, we also discussed that there is a force that is working against that purpose, and that force is sin. Sin separates us from God and creates chaos and confusion making it impossible to accomplish our created purpose on our own. But God, being rich in mercy and love, sent Jesus as the "way, the truth, and the life" so that we could overcome sin through His power and be reconciled back to glorifying His name. The Compartmentalization Conflict is a great diagram that reveals all of this in picture form, therefore, making it easier to grasp and understand. If you are anything like me, I learn better when I see things compared to just hearing.

As humans, we have the tendency to compartmentalize everything in our lives. In other words, we section off or separate certain areas of our lives from other areas. For example, when we go to work, we are focused only on the things that apply to our jobs. When we attend school, we focus on socializing with friends and schoolwork. When we attend a sporting event, our minds and emotions are devoted to rooting for our team. When we go on vacation, we check out from reality and relaxation is our main focus. A more focused example is when we go to the gas station; our minds are focused on getting gas and nothing else. Going to the grocery store is no different; we are in and out after we get what we need. We section off our lives like a checklist and we hop from one box to the next with one desire... to complete the checklist. The problem with this is that worship is slowly being minimized and quarantined to a certain time and place when it was never meant to be. We are called to worship God everywhere always (1 Thess. 5:16-17). The more worship is minimized in the life of the believer, the more ineffective it becomes. Worship was meant to consume our lives, not just be a small part of it.

This seemingly harmless, natural tendency can have some devastating effects on our worship. There is a quote from A.W. Tozer that best sums this idea up. He says, *"That biblically defined purpose is that we might worship God and enjoy Him forever. Apart from that, man has no other purpose; and short of that, man wanders around a spiritual disorientation taking him further from finding his created purpose."*

As we stated earlier, sin confuses us and wants nothing more than to keep us from worshiping God with our entire lives like scripture demands (Romans 12:1, 1 Cor. 10:31, John 4:24, Psalm 145:10). Many times sin does not show up with a huge red flashing light that is obvious to all, but sneaks in quietly and disrupts and disturbs subtly. This can be so much more dangerous in that going undiscovered, sin hangs around longer while slowly hardening the heart of the believer. Over time, it will begin to diminish the desire of the worshiper to worship God and thus, leave him seeking and searching for purpose. Study the diagrams on the next couple of pages and see how compartmentalization can hinder our worship.

<u>Diagram 1</u>: Worship is minimized as a result of sin and compartmentalization.

So, according to scripture and Tozer, the one thing we were created to do, which is worship God with all our "heart, soul, mind, and strength", we are not doing. Sin has deceived us into minimizing worship so that it has now become ineffective. True, genuine worship will always draw the worshiper closer to God and multiply his love for his Maker. It will also testify to the world and unbelievers the immeasurable worth and power of our sovereign Lord and King. Worship sanctifies the believer and evangelizes to the unbeliever. However, when worship is compartmentalized, its life and purpose is sucked out and it becomes nothing more than a song in a service.

Diagram 2: Worship is maximized when it is the center of our life.

worship

Could you imagine how our lives and others around us would change if worship wasn't minimized by compartmentalization, but maximized by the Spirit moving in ALL areas of our lives?

We would see fishing as an opportunity to worship. We would see school as an opportunity for worship. We would see our workplaces and our home life as an opportunity to glorify God. Could you imagine what worship would be like on Sunday mornings if the whole congregation were worshiping like this all week? This is what worship should be. Worship should consume our lives!

Discussion

A) Discuss any moments of challenge, conviction, or encouragement during this week's reading.

B) What are some indicators that you may be compartmentalizing or minimizing worship in your life? Are you complacent? Are you burned out? Are you experiencing a lack of joy in serving?

C) In Philippians 4:4, Paul says, *"Rejoice in the Lord always; again I will say rejoice."* If we compartmentalize and reduce worship to only a few minutes in church every week, it is nearly impossible to live out this verse. When worship consumes our lives, every opportunity becomes an opportunity to worship. Read Acts 16:23-25 and discuss how your response may be different from Paul and Silas' if you were put in the same situation they were.

D) The key to not compartmentalizing our lives and minimizing worship is keeping our eyes fixed on Christ and the things of eternity and not getting distracted by the temporary things of this world (Col. 3:2). In John 15:4, Jesus says, *"Abide in me, and I in you. As the branch cannot bear fruit by itself, unless it abides in the vine, neither can you, unless you abide in me."* Discuss ways we can be intentional about "abiding in Jesus" and keeping worship central in our lives.

Take Away: Worship should consume our lives instead of being constricted by it.

Summary

We must understand that God created us for Himself. His design was for man to know Him and have fellowship with Him while experiencing and responding to His greatness. However, sin has confused man's created purpose and left him searching far and wide to satisfy a desire that can only be fulfilled by knowing and having a relationship with his God and Creator. It is only through Jesus Christ that man's sin can be forgiven and his created purpose, of worshiping God, can fully be restored (Eph. 2:4-7).

Over the past several weeks we have looked fairly deep into our doctrine of God, man, sin, and Jesus knowing that these truths are the foundation of our faith and will continue to shape and mold us as worshipers. We also looked at how sin can deceive us into compartmentalizing our lives to a point where worship is essentially non-existent. Right doctrine will lead us into a more intimate relationship with God and will aid in maximizing worship in our lives. Wrong doctrine will confuse and lead astray. This is why it is so important that sound doctrine be our starting point for leading worship. If our foundation is shaky and unstable, then everything we build on top of it will be shaky and unstable. It is so important that we continue looking to God's Word and His Spirit to reveal to us His Truth. There are countless blogs, articles, books, and voices out there that have wide recognition and huge platforms that have much to say about doctrine and worship. But let me caution you, just because they are on big stages and writing big books doesn't mean they are speaking truth! Always trust God's Word over man's word. I am aware of the irony of that last statement being how I am writing this in hopes to teach, encourage, influence, and inspire. However, I am still being shaped and molded by God's grace and I may not always get it right. You have to trust His Word and His Spirit, for they will never fail.

As worship leaders, we must remember that people are watching us, following us and eventually, will be coming after us to continue our work. What are we leaving them with? What are we teaching them? Where are we leading them? How are we preparing them to succeed in ministry? Paul talks about this in 1 Corinthians 3:10-11 when he speaks of taking great care in laying a firm foundation because he knows people will be following him. There are two things we can take away from this passage. 1) We should be concerned with the spiritual stability of those who will be influenced by us and our ministry. This is why sound doctrine is imperative. 2) We are working on something that is much bigger than ourselves. I heard a quote one time that said, *"Your worship is eternal, but your opportunity to lead isn't."* Hopefully, our ministries and influence will be picked up by the next generation and the Gospel will continue to go forth in our communities changing and transforming lives. We have to keep this mindset as we grow in leadership and influence, otherwise our ministry and influence will die with us. May solid doctrine always be the foundation of our ministries and serve as a tool to strengthen our relationship with the Father.

In this section, **The Worshiper**, we focused on you and your understanding of what worship really is. We highlighted certain truths and beliefs that have to be in line if we are to move forward in leading, teaching, and influencing people for the Kingdom. It is out of our understandings and beliefs that we speak and act. Before moving forward to the next section,

The Worship Leader, take time to reflect and examine your heart as we bring this section to a close.

Psalm 63:1-4 perfectly portrays the heart of the worshiper who finds their greatest sense of satisfaction and completion in knowing God and being in His presence. *Earnestly* the worshiper seeks as his soul *thirsts* for God. You can almost see him looking intently, as if he were studying God, as he beholds His power and His glory. As you read, compare and contrast your worship life with the Psalmist.

"O God, you are my God; earnestly I seek you; my soul thirsts for you; my flesh faints for you, as in a dry and weary land where there is no water. So I have looked upon you in the sanctuary, beholding your power and your glory. Because your steadfast love is better that life; my lips will praise you. So I will bless you as long as I live; in your name I will lift up my hands. " Psalm 63:1-4

Meditation

1) What do you thirst for? What do you earnestly seek after? What do you think about when you wake up and before you go to bed? What drives you?

2) What will it take for worship and bringing glory to God to be the CENTER of your life and not just a part of your life?

Prayer time

1) Pray that God would reveal any sin in your life that may be standing in the way of you desiring to know Him more.

2) Pray that, through the Holy Spirit, God would give you a heart for worship like the Psalmist in Psalm 63.

3) Pray that you would become the worshiper that God has created you to be.

Section 2

The Worship Leader

"We must take the worship-hungry hearts of our congregations and redirect them from seeking after the temporary to being filled, satisfied, and sustained by Jesus and Him alone."

The Worship Leader

While an improper view of worship can have negative effects on a personal level, an improper view of worship leading can have negative effects on a corporate level. When the worshiper steps out from the shadows of their personal time worshiping God and begins to stand before others with the intention of leading, the repercussions of his/her actions and words are greater. The worship leader can help lead others closer to God or further from God. The worship leader can lead people in responding to the truth and the hope of the Gospel or into confusion and chaos. The worship leader can lead others into a greater awareness of God and His presence or into a greater awareness of other idols that are competing for the affections of our hearts. Worship on a personal level has to be steady and grounded before it can be put before the masses. We have to be aware that Satan will be scheming to deceive and searching to destroy even more when we put ourselves in a position of influence over God's Church. This is why we spent five weeks building our foundation of worship

on doctrine. Understanding the role of a worship leader is vital
to creating a culture of awe-inspiring, Holy Spirit-filled,
Christ-centered worship that reflects the power of our God;
instead of the ego-inspiring, flesh-filled, me-centered worship
that reflects the sinfulness of our flesh.

Developing a greater understanding of worship gives us
greater insight as to what exactly the role of a worship leader
is. We desperately need, as worshipers, more clarity on this so
we can better monitor how we are being led. The danger in not
understanding proper worship leading is that the worshiper
may be led unknowingly into participating in improper
worship, or idolatry. A great example of this is found in
Exodus 32. At this time, Moses is spending time with God on
the mountain and the people are becoming restless. They know
they need to worship and they look to Aaron. Aaron knows he
needs to lead them, but obviously isn't sure how. Because of
his and the people's lack of understanding, they engaged in
idol worship, which resulted in them almost being the target of
God's wrath instead of His favor and mercy. I personally don't
think that God's people intended to sin against Him and
worship another, which is the scariest part. *Idol worship isn't
always done knowingly.* We see here that God is very serious
about His people worshiping Him and only Him. Hopefully,
now we are beginning to see the importance of good worship
leaders and the great responsibility they have to lead their
flock well.

Understanding Our Culture

We live in a world today that is drunk on entertainment.
Everywhere we go we want to be entertained. We want to be
impressed. We want to witness things that make our adrenaline

pump, make us feel good, and leave us excited and waiting for more. Just look at the packed out football and baseball stadiums all over our nation. Look at the countless reality TV shows that are so addictive because they feed our appetite for entertainment. Our culture is feeding its people a substance that is fleeting and failing and this is what we are up against as worship leaders. In some cases, we have already seen this appetite for entertainment make its way into the Church. We would rather have a worship leader who can entertain us with his music than challenge and teach us with his mind. We would rather have a worship leader with good hair than a good heart. Many of us think that the key to a dynamic worship service is a cool, hip musician who can "wow" the congregation into coming back week after week with their talents instead of their anointing. Before we can begin to see this culture change, we have to acknowledge that it exists. Instead of feeding in to this false worship, it is our job to redirect it.

We must take the worship hungry hearts of our congregations and redirect them from seeking after the temporary to being filled, satisfied, and sustained by Jesus and Him alone. We must stop focusing on the outward and look at the heart of the one leading us. The Lord warns us of this when He said to Samuel, *"Do not look on his appearance or on the height of his stature, because I have rejected him. For the Lord sees not as man sees: man looks on the outward appearance, but the Lord looks on the heart"* (1 Sam. 16:7). The most important instrument a worship leader has is his heart. In his book *Worship Matters,* Bob Kauflin addresses this same idea. He says, *"God isn't listening to the sound of our music or the quality of our performance. He's hearing the sound of our hearts."*[14]

Understanding Our Tools

Some of the tools the enemy uses to distract our worship are the very ones that we think are helping it. For instance, music can be one of our greatest tools in worship. It speaks a universal language that not only speaks to the mind and intellect through lyrics, but also communicates to the heart and soul through the notes and the melodies. This can be very effective when communicating the Gospel. If not used appropriately, it can be the focus of entertainment instead of a tool for worship. Lighting and media can be used to set an atmosphere and make the congregation feel "connected" to what is going on on-stage; but if the worship leader doesn't intentionally use these tools to magnify the greatness of God instead of the "coolness" of man, we are aiding in idol worship. Gear is another tool that can be the focus of too much attention by the musicians using them. I feel like I see more worship leaders talking about gear, tone, and equipment than about Jesus. Another example is our traditions. Routines are good for encouraging participation and keeping the people engaged, but when they become the focus over desiring to encounter God each week, we are aiding in idol worship. Many times in our services, too much emphasis is placed on one individual. Whether it is the one on-stage who we have given the "rock star" status, or the one sitting in the congregation who thinks the entire service revolves around him and his preferences. We have to be aware and sober to all the ways the enemy can twist and pervert our worship so we will not directly or indirectly, place the focus on lesser things.

The sobering reality is that we live in a world that is trying desperately to steal our worship. Much like Satan desired to rob God of His glory and worship, our sinful world today is trying to pull worshipers away from God and towards sin. Our sinful flesh is trying to convince us that it is more satisfying to please ourselves than to please our Father. The darkness is relentlessly trying to drown out the light with lies and deception. Paul describes it best in Ephesians 6:12 when he says, *"For we do not wrestle against flesh and blood, but against the rulers, against the authorities, against the cosmic powers over this present darkness, against the spiritual forces of evil in the heavenly places."* This battle is going on for the souls of man all around us everyday and that puts worship leaders on the front lines. The people of our congregations are in this battle and most of them don't even know it. One of the main roles of the worship leader is to realize this battle and lead and prepare the people to fight it.

Now, with all that said, the purpose of this next section is to give us the insight and direction we need, as worship leaders, to keep from leading our congregations astray. We have been given a great task and opportunity that must be treated with humility and respect. In this next section, we will recap from the last section on our understanding of worship and discuss some common misconceptions of worship leading. We will also be focusing much of our time on the heart of the worship leader for we know that *"out of the abundance of the heart the mouth speaks"* (Matt. 12:34). We will start right now by defining the term "worship leader" based on all that we have discussed so far. Here is an extensive, accurate, and focused definition of a worship leader. *A worship leader uses their gifts and abilities to help redirect the focus of the worshiping heart away from the created, temporary things that do not satisfy, to God, the Creator of all things who will eternally satisfy, by pointing to Jesus and the cross.*

Week 6

The ABC's
of Worship Leading

"So worship is much more than the songs we sing or the music we play. The songs should be an overflow of our worship, not our worship in its entirety."

The ABC's of
Worship Leading

As we continue to progress in our understanding of worship and worship leading, it is essential for us to be well informed of the exact purpose of our worship times. We are given a responsibility to lead people. How can we lead them well if there is question or uncertainty in our hearts about what we are doing and why? The truth is that we can't. We will just drag them along the way as we seek to find and discover that hidden place called worship. At best, they will be unmoved and unchanged, and at worst, we will lead them to worship false gods. We must be worshipers BEFORE we are worship leaders. Knowing that the goal of our worship time is a greater awareness of God and His glory, while all lesser gods are pushed back as we fix our hearts and minds on Him, is imperative. This is why we sing! We sing to remind us of what Jesus has done for us. We sing to remember His faithfulness and goodness in times of hurt and suffering. We sing to respond to God's love, grace, mercy, and truth in our lives. We sing to teach our hearts more about His character. We sing to draw near to Him (Psalm 145:18, James 4:8), and we sing to see Him increase and us decrease (John 3:30).

This week we are going to go over some foundational truths about what worship is and what it is not. Hopefully focusing on these issues and thoughtfully reading through them will bring some clarity to us and in turn, will help us be more effective when leading. Here are some basic truths about worship.

Worship Is A Lifestyle

"I appeal to you therefore, brothers, by the mercies of God, to present your bodies as a living sacrifice, holy and acceptable to God, which is your spiritual worship." Romans 12:1

Worship is our daily response to God. It is our response to His greatness, His sufficiency, His unfailing love, His faithfulness, His grace, His forgiveness, and even His discipline. It is the constant acknowledgement of His lordship over our lives every second of every day. We are to live our lives in a continual state of thanksgiving and appreciation for who God is and what He has done for us. The songs we sing are meaningless if our lives aren't singing them first. The works we do are meaningless if are hearts aren't doing them to glorify God. *"Imitate God, therefore, in everything you do, because you are His dear children. Live a life filled with love, following the example of Christ."(Eph. 5:1-2)*

Everyday we are faced with the decision to allow our worship to be shaped by lesser gods. This starts with our sinful nature telling us that we exist to serve and worship ourselves. This self-worship, or idol worship, is reinforced everywhere we turn in our society. We see it in our television shows and movies. We see it in our music and entertainment. We see it in the news and in the media. Everywhere we look our worship, and our lives, are being shaped by someone or something. Our job, as worship leaders, is to let the truth of who God is, instead of the lies of this world, shape the worship of His people. This is an everyday battle that we must empower our congregations to fight. So worship is much more than the songs we sing or the music we play. The songs should be an overflow of our worship, not our worship in its entirety. It is the laying down of our lives for the glory of God. In everything we do and say, we glorify Him (1 Cor. 10:31).

Worship Involves Our Entire Being

"You must love the Lord your God with all your heart, all your soul, all your mind, and all your strength." Mark 12:30

What we love the most and what we think about most often is what we will eventually end up worshiping. Worship is the overflow of the heart, so when our hearts and our minds are filled with love for God, then we will worship Him the way He desires. As true followers of Christ, we must look at Jesus' life and strive to follow in His footsteps. Jesus was completely consumed with love for His Father (John 14:31). We see that in everything He said, thought, and did He was obedient to the

Father revealing His undivided love and devotion to Him. We are called to love God with the same passion and abandonment that Jesus did. We should worship and honor God with everything that we love. We should glorify Him and seek to please Him with not only the words we speak, but also every thought we think. We should magnify His greatness with everything we put effort into such as work, relationships, music, sports, etc. The key to doing this is abiding in Him (John 15:4) by reading His word and staying in constant fellowship with Him through prayer.

Worship that is acceptable to God is all or nothing. He will not accept partial worship or worship that is divided between idols. We saw this example in Exodus when the Israelites worshiped the golden calf. We also see God's anger towards worship that is not centered on Him in Amos 5:23 when He says, *"Take away from me the noise of your songs; to the melody of your harps I will not listen."* The heart, soul, mind, and body are a package that makes up the complete being of a person. Our entire being, every part of who we are, should love God completely. In order for true worship to occur, all parts have to work together. Anything less is lukewarm and God despises lukewarm worship (Rev. 3:16).

We Worship God Through Jesus Christ

"Jesus said to him, "I am the way, and the truth, and the life. No one comes to the Father except through me." John 14:6

Jesus is our Savior and Redeemer and apart from Him we remain dead in our sin and separated from God. Through the shedding of His blood on the cross and His resurrection, we have been reconciled back to the Father (Romans 5:1). Because the curse of sin and death has been defeated (Col. 2: 13-15). There is no other name, work, or belief system that can accomplish this for us. It is because of Christ, and Christ alone, that we have the opportunity to experience true forgiveness and eternal salvation. God is not impressed with our works or best efforts (Isaiah 64:6), but only the perfect work of Jesus. Without believing in Jesus as Lord and trusting Him with our lives, it is impossible for us to worship God. So, in essence, only believers can worship God. Non-believers can be affected and impacted by our worship, but they cannot worship God appropriately without Jesus as their mediator. *"For there is only one God and one Mediator who can reconcile God and humanity – the man Christ Jesus." - 1 Tim. 2:5*

Worship Is Not For Us

"Not to us, O Lord, not to us, but to your name give glory, for the sake of your steadfast love and your faithfulness!" Psalm 115:1

Worship was created for God and not for us. It's purpose is to please Him. It's end is to glorify Him. Worship was designed with God as the author and the center. He is the only worthy object of worship because He is the only one that can carry the weight of being worshiped. Everything and everyone else will eventually break under the weight of something only meant to be carried by the divine. When true Godly worship takes place, our personal wants and desires begin to align with

God's as the Holy Spirit sanctifies our lives by ridding us from the sin that corrupts it. Differences we face today like whether a church is traditional or contemporary in its presentation of the Gospel, or what style of music is played for worship becomes irrelevant when the presence of the Living God shows up. Our styles and preferences are different because we are different. However, our God is bigger than the generational gaps and cultural barriers that so often separate us as believers. We cannot let something that is supposed to be all about God become all about us. Worship was not created for our benefit or to give us pleasure. But, when we worship Him in spirit and in truth (John 4:24) and with clean hands and pure hearts (Psalm 24: 3-4), He does reveal Himself to us and we are filled and satisfied (Psalm 107:9). *"When we draw near to God, He draws near to us." (James 4:8)*

Worship Is Not Confined

"Let the message about Christ, in all it's richness, fill your lives. Teach and counsel each other with all the wisdom He gives. Sing psalms and hymns and spiritual songs to God with thankful hearts. And whatever you do or say, do it as a representative of the Lord Jesus giving thanks through Him to God the Father." Colossians 3:16-17

Since worship is a lifestyle, it is not confined to anything. It is not confined to a certain building, time of the week, or setting. Worship is not confined to our stylistic preferences such as traditional or contemporary. Worship is not confined to playing music, or not playing music. Any believer can worship in any setting at any time. Jesus was communicating this truth to the woman at the well in John 4:23-24. He says, *"But the hour is coming, and is now here, when the true worshippers will worship the Father in spirit and truth, for the Father is seeking such people to worship Him. God is spirit and those who worship Him must worship in spirit and truth."* This is good for all worship leaders and musicians to hear. Our gifts aren't essential for worship to take place. They only aid and encourage worship when used appropriately. When we begin to focus too much on practices, preferences, and traditions, the object of our worship becomes the created instead of the Creator (Romans 1:22-23).

Discussion

A) Discuss any moments of challenge, conviction, or encouragement during this week's reading.

B) We stated earlier that worship is "not just a song, but it is a lifestyle." The songs are merely the tools we use to accomplish the greater task of inspiring and encouraging our congregations to live lives of worship to a Holy and a Righteous God. How does this change the way we lead? We are not out to entertain or impress, but to inspire and encourage people to "walk by the spirit and not by the flesh" (Gal. 5:16).

C) We also stated earlier that worship "is not for us." We were never intended to be the focus of worship, but in many churches we are. Sometimes I think we put too much focus on relating to or pleasing the people we are before, instead of leading them to please God through lifting up the name of Jesus. Jesus alone has the power to save (John 12:32) so why would we center our worship services around anything else like popular songs or cool gimmicks that have nothing to do with Jesus? Do we really trust the Holy Spirit to do His job of convicting the world of sin and leading us into the Truth (John 16:8-14)? Do we really trust that as we lift up Christ and worship Him alone, that the Holy Spirit is capable of transforming the hearts of unbelievers and shallow believers?

D) Acceptable worship is more about the heart than anything else. If our hearts are sinful, then our worship is unacceptable. If our hearts are on Jesus, then our worship will be pleasing to the Lord (Matt. 12:33-35). The truth is that all things can be used to please God and honor Him; the problem is when we misuse them for our selfish desires. *"For everything created by God is good, and nothing is to be rejected if it is received with thanksgiving, for it is made holy by the word of God and prayer" (1 Tim. 4:4-5).* Discuss how this affects the accountability and responsibility we have to continue to keep the focus on Christ as we use various media and tools such as technology (internet, facebook, twitter), media (lighting, videos), and music in our worship services.

Take Away: We must be worshipers before we are worship leaders.

Week 7

Misconceptions about Worship Leading

"As a result, we have created a culture of worship ministry in our churches that is very man-centered. The only problem is that man can't purify hearts and redeem souls."

Misconceptions about Worship Leading

Everything we have discussed thus far, every worship leader should already be familiar with. It is essential and foundational. However, I have seen a growing shift in the culture of worship leading in churches over the past several years. It is a culture that is breeding an entitlement mentality among musicians and people on stage. It is communicating that the musicians' skills and time are of more importance than the countless others who volunteer every week. I am not saying that the musicians aren't important because they are. They are extremely important to the presentation of the Gospel in the service each week. However, so are the skills and time of the greeters, the security team, the welcome team, the coffee team, the prayer team, the childcare teams, etc. The list goes on and on. Music is important, but it is not the only thing that happens that impacts people for Christ each week.

I feel it is important to address some of these misconceptions and mentalities that are lurking in the hearts of our worship teams today. My goal is not to offend or call anyone out. My goal is only to inform so that we can be aware. If we are not aware, then how can we begin to correct or solve the problem? I don't think these mindsets are intentional or malicious in any way, in fact, it is a product of what our leadership seems to be creating by placing the "production" of worship over the "heart" of worship. By this, we are communicating to our churches that God accepts our worship on the basis of our skill instead of the condition of our heart. Many worship leaders feel pressured to execute flawless sets every week because their pastors are expecting it. As a result, we have created a culture of worship ministry in our churches that is very man-centered. The only problem is that man can't purify hearts and redeem souls.

Pay to Play

This is a topic that is widely debated amongst some of the godliest leaders in our churches today and both sides have valid points. It is on the issue of paying musicians to play each week. We have to start this conversation because if we proceed here without using wisdom and good judgement, creating a culture where musicians expect a paycheck for their services on Sunday, can be very harmful to our ministries and even our churches. It may not be harmful externally in terms of production and musicianship, but as we have established, true worship is about much more than that. Establishing leaders and putting people in an area of influence based solely on their skill, instead of their heart, is dangerous. Worship leaders and those leading on stage should be serving and sacrificing for their church. They should know the people they are leading and they should be committed to the vision of the church. They should be using their gifts to serve just like every other volunteer.

The problem isn't necessarily with paying musicians or not paying musicians. I understand that each church is different and some have more resources than others, which enable them to do more for their volunteers. I also understand that money is not the potential problem here... it is the love of money (1 Tim. 6:10). However, if we choose to venture into this territory as we build our ministry, we must be aware and alert to the possible negative effects that could arise.

Paying our worship teams to play every Sunday could encourage a culture where there is no accountability and no responsibility for those on-stage. It could also encourage resentment and bitterness with other volunteers who may not be getting paid for their service. It could breed a culture of entitlement and competition among the musicians within the worship ministry. It could communicate that worship is nothing more than a gig or a paycheck. It could communicate that God is more pleased with our worship based on the quality of our performance. It could communicate to others that their gift isn't good enough or great enough to lead others in worship.

Again, money is not the root of all these issues. At the end of the day, it is sin that causes them all and that is a battle we will continue to fight. What we must understand as worship leaders, is that it is our responsibility to make wise judgments and to do our very best to shepherd the hearts of not only our congregations, but those who serve along-side us each week. I don't think it is wrong to appreciate, provide for, and/or compensate in any way the people who are regularly serving week in and week out. We should always appreciate our volunteers and leaders. And I also understand that from time to time a musician may need to be brought in to fill a gap somewhere or give our regulars a break. These things are all realities in maintaining the consistency in our ministry and need to be done from time to time. However, I feel that if and when we choose to compensate, we must proceed with caution and wisdom for our ministry should be built firmly on the foundation of humility, service, and sacrifice. Satan will use anything to corrupt and pollute the hearts of our worship leaders.

Later we will look at some of the greatest worship leaders in scripture who gave up everything for the sake of the Gospel. Moses, David, Jesus, John, Paul. None of these guys, except David, were musicians but they lead people in worship with their lives. True worship leading that we see from these guys in scripture reveals humility, responsibility, service, and sacrifice. Pride, arrogance, and entitlement have no place in leading worship. Here are some common misconceptions in our culture today about worship leading.

1. Worship leading is not a gig. It is a responsibility.

No one understands this concept more than Moses. After being called out and set apart by God to lead His people out of Egypt, despite a little hesitation and uncertainty, Moses fully commits himself and takes responsibility. He commits to God. He commits to the people. And he commits to the task. We see this in his faithfulness and perseverance not only in times of blessing and provision, but also in the face of resistance and rejection (Ex. 7:4-6, Ex. 16:2-3). He loved God and he loved the people and he understood his responsibility to both. Too many worship leaders today want the influence of the stage without the responsibility that comes with it: the responsibility of leadership. Worship leading is about understanding the responsibility to care, protect, teach, guide, and lead the people while being faithful and obedient to God. We can't do this if we don't know them or invest in them. When we abandon the people for the production of our music and the recognition of our position, our impact and influence for the Gospel will be as temporary as the songs we sing.

2. Worship leading is not a right. It is a privilege.

One thing we must realize as we continue to grow as worship leaders is that we do not have this position or title because we deserve it or earned it. None of us deserve to worship God, much less lead others in worship. He has enabled us to know Him and to lead others to know Him. There are too many worship leaders who are leading their bands and congregations out of an attitude of entitlement. For example, phrases like "I earned this" or "I deserve this" are common thoughts in the minds of these worship leaders. This attitude focuses the attention on the wrong person. The truth is we don't have anything that wasn't given to us first; so then, how can we say we earned it (1 Cor. 4:7). God is not impressed with our gifts or talents because He is the one who gave them to us. He is impressed

with seeing Christ in us and Christ exalted by our gifts.
All throughout scripture we see that God uses those
who rely on His strength and power instead of their
own (1 Cor. 1:26-31).

3. Worship leading is about decreasing, not increasing.

It is very easy to let the power of a position or the
influences of success go to our heads. If we are not
careful, we will begin to place ourselves on a pedestal
and build a ministry that revolves around our egos,
instead of Christ. We will soon begin taking from God
what is rightfully His: the worship and praise of His
people. We can learn a lot from John the Baptist. His
whole ministry and purpose was to point to someone
else, someone greater (John 1:23). His desire and his
role were to prepare the stage for Christ. Shouldn't that
be ours as well? Shouldn't our responsibility be to
deflect all the attention and recognition we receive to
someone/something greater... like the Gospel? Jesus
says in Matthew 18:4 that *"Whoever humbles himself
like this child is the greatest in the kingdom of
heaven."* We know that Jesus is the greatest example
of humility for He *"made Himself nothing"*
(Philippians 2:7) and came to earth to be obedient to
the Father and point people to Him. We must be the
first to empty ourselves out and always deflect the
attention we receive to Jesus. We can only do this as
He becomes bigger and we become smaller. We are
His instruments and nothing more (Romans 6:13). True
worship leading leaves the people more amazed by a
great God rather than a leader's great gifts!

4. Worship leading isn't just singing songs. It is declaring war.

Anytime we openly declare our love, adoration, and allegiance to God, we are raising a battle cry in defiance to His enemy. We have already discussed that there is a battle going on for the souls of man. Satan is attempting to steal God's worship and deceive and disrupt His will in the lives of His people (John 10:10). The greatest weapon we have to fight this battle is worship. There is nothing more powerful than the worship of God's people. Jehoshaphat witnessed this first hand when he placed his musicians before his army as they marched into battle (2 Chron. 20) as the Lord had instructed him to do. As the musicians lead in worship, God destroyed the enemies. Wow! This story will never get old for me. God was making a statement here. If we trust him and find our delight in Him, He will fight our battles (2 Chron. 20:17). Just think that as we engage in worship, the Holy Spirit is engaging in warfare on our behalf. *"Let the high praise of God be in their throats and two-edged swords in their hands." (Psalm 149:5)*

5. Worship leading isn't just the calling of one, but of every believer.

Every believer in Christ has the responsibility and calling to lead others in worship. Paul tells us that we are *"ambassadors for Christ. God making His appeal through us" (2 Chron. 5:20)*. We all have an audience, no matter who we are or what we do. Teachers have students. Parents have children. Coaches have players.

Bosses have employees. Friends have other friends. What would they say is important to us? What would they say we love the most? What would they say we worship? Our universal calling as believers is to live lives that point people to Christ. *"In the same way, let your light shine before others, so that they may see your good works and give glory to your Father who is in heaven." (Matt. 5:16)*

Discussion

A) Discuss any moments of challenge, conviction, or encouragement during this week's reading.

B) Discuss the dangers of establishing a culture where all the musicians are paid to serve on Sundays, but other volunteers aren't. What is that communicating to the other teams? How could this negatively affect their attitude to serve? It is very easy for us to be so focused on our ministry that we neglect considering and encouraging others. Read Hebrews 12:14-15. This is our responsibility as we labor for the Gospel!

C) 1 Corinthians 4:7 says, *"For who sees anything different in you? What do you have that you did not receive? If then you received it, why do you boast as if you did not receive it?"* Think back on how God has provided gifts, situations, opportunities, and/or people in your life to place you in the position you are in. Now, think of all the mechanics, waiters/waitresses, lawyers, trash collectors, accountants, landscapers, builders, etc. that may have been great musicians or worship leaders, but never had the opportunities you had. How does this make you appreciate the opportunity to lead more when you realize that it was given to you?

D) John 3:30 says, *"He must increase, but I must decrease."* Do you have a hard time WANTING to deflect the praise and attention of man to Jesus? Anyone can do it, but not everyone wants to. Do you have a hard time wanting to see those around you increase, instead of you? For instance, other musicians or worship leaders. Do you find it hard to put others in the spotlight? John was always pointing to Christ and so should we. Jesus was always pouring into and raising up His disciples to eventually do even greater things than He did (John 14:12). These are questions we must answer. If we are not okay with decreasing, then worship leading is not for us.

Take Away: Our worship ministry, inside and out, should always reflect the character and heart of Christ.

Week 8

The heart

"Our heart is the place where our passion dwells and our conviction speaks. It is the place where honesty is the only reality. Our heart is the place where everything we care about and hold dear is kept. It is the place where worship flows."

The Heart of Worship Leading

We have been focusing hard on the heart of the worship leader because honestly, this is what is on display each week. Our heart is the place where our passion dwells and our conviction speaks. It is the place where honesty is the only reality. Our heart is the place where everything we care about and hold dear is kept. It is the place where worship flows.

God delights in our hearts

God does not delight in our songs alone or our voices. He is not pleased merely with our talents or our traditions. We can learn how to be spiritual in front of others and impress them with our acts, but if our hearts aren't flowing with adoration and allegiance to Jesus than none of it matters to God. We can fool others, but we can't fool Him. Jesus spoke about this heartless worship in Matthew 15:8-9. He says, *"This people honors me with their lips, but their heart is far from me; in vain do they worship me, teaching as doctrines the commandments of men."* God delights in those whose hearts are set on and consumed with Him (Matt. 5:8). He delights in the heart that pursues after Him over all other things because it knows that He alone is greater (John 8:12). He delights in the heart that is eternally satisfied in Him and needs no other (John 4:14).

There is so much emphasis placed on the heart in scripture because, for the believer, that is where Christ dwells. Not in our physical heart, but in our desires, passions, and longings. All these things that used to be controlled by our sinful flesh have now been overtaken by Jesus and our hearts have been made new (2 Cor. 5:17). Now, the love of Christ is not only a part of us, but it controls us (2 Cor. 514). And when a heart is controlled and consumed by Jesus, great things happen. Eternal things happen. *"Whoever believes in me, as the Scripture has said, "Out of his heart will flow rivers of living water." (John 7:38)*

This is where we should desire to be as worship leaders. This is where we need to be if we want our congregations to encounter Jesus each week and be impacted by God's eternal love and grace. This week we will discuss how worship leaders must have a heart for God, a heart for the flock, a heart to teach, and a heart to serve.

A Heart For God

"One thing have I asked of the Lord, that will I seek after: that I may dwell in the house of the Lord all the days of my life, to

gaze upon the beauty of the Lord and to inquire in His temple." Psalm 27:4

Our passion for knowing God and being near to Him must be supreme in our lives. One of the greatest worshipers of all time who was described as a "man after God's own heart" was David (Acts 13:22). David desired more than anything to be in the presence of the Lord (Psalm 27:4, Psalm 24:3-4) and his love for God is revealed in every Psalm that he wrote. He speaks of not "wanting" for anything and being "restored" and fulfilled as he "dwells in the house of the Lord forever" in Psalm 23. David's overflowing heart of thankfulness and praise can be seen in Psalm 103:1 as he commands his entire being to worship. *"Bless the Lord, O my soul, and all that is within me, bless His holy name."* He also relied on God's providence and trusted in God's power in times of uncertainty in Psalm 20:7-8 when he says, *"Some trust in chariots and some in horses, but we trust in the name of the Lord our God. They collapse and fall, be we rise and stand upright."* David did not develop this heart for God over night, but through a lifetime of fellowshipping with his Creator. David's heart was consumed with love for God.

Many worship leaders confuse their love for music or performance with love for God. This can happen so easily as we desire to please God by giving Him the best of everything we have. We practice longer, work harder, and buy bigger and better equipment in our pursuit of excellence. Desiring to give God our best and being excellent while doing it is not a bad thing unless it takes priority over knowing and spending time with Him. This is evident when the amount of time preparing the music, rehearsing the songs, and perfecting the presentation far outweighs the amount of time spent with God preparing the heart. It is very easy to think just because we are passionate about the "act" of worship that means we are passionate about the "source" of worship as well. This isn't always the case. We must always be examining our hearts and evaluating our motives when we are planning a set or leading a set. What a person loves the most is what they will worship (Matt. 6:21).

A Heart For The Flock

"I am the good shepherd. I know my own and my own know me, just as the Father knows me and I know the Father; and I lay down my life for the sheep." John 10:14-15

The reason any leader leads is in hopes that people will follow. Much like Moses, we are looking to God to use us to lead people out of various types of bondage and into His rest. Disbelief, doubt, fear, pride, anger, jealousy, unforgiveness, and adultery are just the tip of the iceberg. Hopefully our doctrine is sound and our hearts are pure so we will not lead them astray, but the reality is that people will not follow us if they don't trust us. And people don't trust someone they don't know.

One of the greatest foreshadowings of what Christ would come to do for us is found in the Old Testament. God chooses Moses to lead His people out of bondage and slavery in Egypt and into the Promised Land. For the most part, Moses was a very effective leader because he had a heart for the people. Moses cared for them because he knew them. He was close to them. He was one of them. He shared in their burdens (Ex. 5:4). He shared in their frustrations and pains (Ex. 5:22-23).

He faced fear and opposition with them (Ex. 14) and he rejoiced with them (Ex. 15). Moses witnessed many mighty acts performed by the Lord with the people (Ex. 16&17). And this is the biggest one of all. Moses did not abandon his people in their disobedience! He pleaded to God on their behalf (Ex. 32:11-14). Both Moses and Jesus knew how important it was to have a heart for the people they were leading. They were shepherds and understood that the shepherd exists to serve the flock; the flock doesn't exist to serve the shepherd.

Sadly, we are seeing a generation of worship leaders who would rather lead from a distance. They would rather stay where everything is safe and clean, than get up close and personal like Moses and Jesus did. Here, they don't have to get involved with people's problems and hang-ups. They also don't have to invest in something or someone if they don't feel like it. This isn't the case for all, but many are leading worship for the way it can benefit them, instead of how it will benefit the people.

Worship leading starts off the stage, meaning it starts with a heart for God and a heart for His people. The ability to lead, influence, and have the trust of a congregation doesn't come with a title or a position. It develops when the people see that the worship leader has a heart for them and is invested in them. In John 10:14, we see that Jesus knows and is known by His sheep. As a result, the sheep hear His voice and follow Him because they trust Him. In stark contrast, the "hired hand" cares nothing for the flock and is serving only out of selfish gain, a paycheck. In verse 13, we see how damaging this can be when the hired hand abandons the flock when they need him most because he has nothing invested in them. We need more shepherds in our churches and less hired hands.

A Heart To Teach

"Him we proclaim, warning everyone and teaching everyone with all wisdom, that we may present everyone mature in Christ." Colossians 1:28

Our greatest responsibility as shepherds, leaders, pastors, and even believers is to "go and make disciples" (Matt. 28:19). It is not to please our hearers and be everyone's best friend. Nor is it to have a lot of fans and build the largest church in the area. Our job is to go and be Jesus' witnesses preaching and teaching through His power unto all the earth (Acts 1:8). We have been placed in a position of influence and as "good stewards"(1 Cor. 4:1-2) of that influence, we must teach, equip, and instruct our congregations in the same way Jesus did. His entire ministry was spent teaching on who God was, who He was, and what He came to do. Satan will use anything he can to deceive us and pull us away from worshiping God. One of the biggest and most effective tools he has is ignorance. Jesus understood this better than anyone and He knew that the best defense against ignorance is knowledge.

This is exactly why we started this book off with several weeks of doctrine. It is imperative that we understand The Gospel completely and can communicate it clearly because the Gospel is what people need. It is what brings hope and light to those who feel lost and hopeless. It is what saves, and people can't respond to it if they don't know it. A true worship leader finds greater joy in seeing the church grow in faith and spiritual maturity than he does in executing the perfect worship set.

As worship leaders, we have many details to consider each week as we try to eliminate all possible distractions in our services, so that the Gospel will be seen and heard clearly by all. Some of these include planning the set, scheduling and rehearsing with the band, making sure all media is ready, making sure that lighting is conducive for worship, and that there is a flow of worship that keeps people engaged. There are many other technical issues that seem to spring up every week with the equipment that must be attended too. My point is that it would be very easy to stay busy "putting on" worship every week; but we must not lose sight of our long-term responsibility in the face of the more short-term ones. That responsibility is to teach and proclaim Christ in everything we do so that we may present all those given to us mature in Christ (Col. 1:28). This heart to teach is revealed in Jesus when He calls His disciples to *come* and follow Him (Matt. 4:19). I don't think it is a coincidence that this was one of the first things He did when His ministry started. Jesus understood the importance and necessity for teaching truth in a world that so desperately needs it. We see this same desire to teach in Paul as he tells the Corinthians to *"Be imitators of me, as I am of Christ." (1 Cor. 10:33)*

A Heart To Serve

"For even the Son of Man came not to be served but to serve, and to give his life as a ransom for many." Mark 10:45

We have already discussed this topic several times, but I believe that it can never be overemphasized. Worship leaders must have a true desire to serve and to pour themselves out for the sake of God being magnified in the lives of His people. The greatest example of this willingness to be emptied out is revealed when Jesus comes to earth in obedience to His Father to do for us what we could never do for ourselves (Philippians 2:6-8). If there was anyone who ever had an excuse to pull rank and demand to be served, it was Jesus. However, He didn't because He was setting the example for us.

Another great example of a heart to serve is found in John the Baptist. His entire ministry revolved around preparing the way and supporting someone else... Jesus (John 1:6-8). When asked about his identity, he immediately states that he "is not the Christ" (John 1:20) which meant he had enough notoriety and recognition for people to think he was. When Jesus shows up on the scene, John begins publicly praising Him and directing people's attention to Him (John 1:29-30). If that wasn't enough, John loses two of his own disciples when they leave him to go and follow Jesus (John 1:35:37). This is an extreme WOW moment for me. John did the best thing he could for those two guys by teaching them about Christ and acknowledging His presence when He showed up. Isn't that ultimately our job as leaders? Shouldn't we be teaching and proclaiming Christ to all under our care and leading them to follow Him when He shows up? Shouldn't we be decreasing as He is increasing (John 3:30)?

There is definitely a battle of "flesh" versus "spirit" here. Our flesh tells us that leaders don't serve, but rather, are served. Our world tells us that power means privilege and those on the top shouldn't mix with those on the bottom. God's word tells us something completely different. It tells us that the "last shall be first, and the first shall be last" (Matt. 20:16) and that we should "count others more significant than ourselves" (Philippians 2:3-4). Like John, the heart of the worship leader should desire to see Christ lifted up not only in his own life, but also in his ministry and in his church. We can never forget that our job is to always point to someone greater... Jesus.

Discussion

A) Discuss any moments of challenge, conviction, or encouragement during this week's reading.

B) How aware are we of God's power and presence each week in our services? Do we feel as though we NEED God to go before us or have we become comfortable going without Him? These are super convicting questions that we must answer. Read Exodus 33:15-16 and examine Moses' heart for God. What does Moses say will distinguish him and his people from all others on earth in verse 16? How does this impact you as one who is leading God's people as well?

C) Jesus says in John 10:4-5 that "...*the sheep follow him, for they know his voice. A stranger they will not follow, but they will flee from him, for they do not know the voice of stranger.*" Building the trust of your flock takes work and it takes time. What are some practical things you can do to help get to know your flock and help your flock get to know you?

D) Read 1Timothy 4:13-16. Teaching is not just a suggestion, but a necessity and the benefits of it can be substantial and eternal (v16). What are some ways you can be intentional about teaching as you lead? A saying our worship team says a lot is, "Our songs are our sermons." This saying holds us accountable and keeps us focused on teaching our congregations through our music. So, just like the preacher is communicating certain truths and points in his sermon, we should be communicating certain truths and attributes of God as well in our songs.

E) In John 4, Jesus encounters the woman at the well. This is such a great example of serving because Jesus had been ministering nonstop and came to the well to have a rest (John 4:6) and to take a break. His disciples had left Him alone so no one would know if Jesus just decided to let this woman get her water and leave. But He didn't. He was intentional about speaking to her. Breaking all kinds of cultural barriers at the time, He continued to serve when it would have been easier not to. As a result, *"Many Samaritans from that town believed in Him because of the woman's testimony (John 4:39)*. We have an incredible opportunity each week in our services as our communities are "coming to the well" to find salvation. Are we serving and making the most of that opportunity like Jesus, or are we letting people walk by because we are too busy?

Take Away: There is only one thing worse than an out of tune instrument during worship and that's an out of tune heart.

Week 9

The Art of Worship Leading

"As we continue to grow and mature as leaders, we must understand that it is our responsibility to set the example of excellence, and excellence doesn't just happen. It is found in the details."

The Art of Worship Leading

Believe it or not, there is an art to worship leading. By art, I mean certain disciplines that we should practice that will make us more effective and efficient as we communicate to people. How we engage people and how we relate to them plays an important role in how they respond to our leadership. Even Jesus had an art to how He communicated to people. Sometimes He spoke with compassion and gentleness, and other times He spoke with sternness and rebuke. Sometimes He chose to pray privately, but other times He chose to pray publicly so that those around Him could hear His heart. Sometimes He taught using words, and other times He taught using acts. Sometimes He spoke very directly, and other times He spoke in parables. We so often just focus on *what* Jesus taught, instead of also focusing on *how* He taught.

This is a very important piece of the puzzle that could potentially be the difference in seeing people move from not participating and responding in worship, to fully engaging and actively being involved in worship. I know in light of everything we have been talking about up until this point, this seems very shallow and unspiritual. However, when we step out in obedience and start leading people, we are responsible for them and should be evaluating every aspect of our leadership. We must ask ourselves questions like: What am I directly communicating with my words and my songs? What am I indirectly communicating with my actions and my demeanor? Are my actions and demeanor lining up with my words and my songs? These are the intricate details that are so important to people not only hearing the Gospel each week, but seeing it as well.

A God of Details

Our God is definitely a God of details. We see this over and over again in scripture. He chose to systematically create the universe and the earth instead of simply making it all appear at once. He was concerned with the roles and the boundaries for Adam and Eve in the Garden (Gen. 2:15-17), He was concerned with the measurements and dimensions of Noah's ark (Gen. 6:14-22), He was concerned with the details of how His people were to act and interact with Him (Ex. 20, Ex. 25-30). He was even concerned with the details of the magnificence of His Temple because His Temple declared His greatness and superiority to the world (2 Chron. 2:5). Our God is a God of details and what we can learn from Him is that the details are important. Excellence is found in the details. If we want to strive to not only *give* our best to God but *be* our best for Him; we must be concerned with the details as well.

A big mistake many worship leaders make is under-emphasizing the practical things that go along with leading a team. These things are necessary for eliminating confusion and keeping everyone connected and informed so the team can function as a unit instead of as individuals. Communication, planning, and preparation are the main ingredients needed to ensure that the team is effective at impacting our audiences with the good news of the Gospel. As we continue to grow and mature as leaders, we must understand that it is our responsibility to set the example of excellence, and excellence doesn't just happen. It is found in the details. We should also strive to push those around us to pursue excellence as well. God does not expect mediocrity. He expects excellence. Excellence in our planning. Excellence in our practicing. And excellence in our performing. He expects excellence because He is excellent. His magnificent temple reflected and represented His greatness to the world in the Old Testament, and now we are that temple (1 Cor. 6:19). Our responsibility is to do the same. We should magnify His excellence with our lives. We strive for excellence not because we want more recognition or praise for our efforts, but because we serve a most excellent God who has given us the most excellent message to share!

However, there is great danger in pursuing excellence on the stage without pursuing excellence off the stage. In other words, we strive to give God our best in public, without giving Him our best in private. This is called *putting the art before the heart*. The art is only as powerful as the heart is humble. Without a pure heart for worship driving the motives and actions of the worship leader, the art of leading just becomes a charade that leads everyone astray. Both are essential and both are important, but the heart of worship must always come before the art of worship. This week we will be focusing on the practical things that will make our worship leading more clear and effective while creating a joyful and stress-free environment for our teams to serve in. We will discuss things such as planning, preparing, presence, and breaking through the wall. All these play an essential role in establishing common ground with our congregations and engaging them with the message of the Gospel. They will also help free the worship leader up to keep his focus on the Lord and during worship instead of being distracted by everything else. Just remember as we go through this week, the heart must come before the art!

Planning

Planning is one of the most practical things a worship leader will do and definitely, the least exciting. Many worship leaders are by nature, very creative and free spirited, and the idea of planning can often times cause friction with our spontaneous side. We feel like planning will take the heart, or life, out of our worship leading. Many of us have a hard time planning because we truly want to leave room for the unknown and leave space for the Holy Spirit to move. Too much planning can confine everyone, including the Holy Spirit, and quench any idea of spontaneity in our services. However, not enough planning will most likely lead to confusion, mediocrity, a frustrated team, and an unresponsive congregation. The reason many of us struggle with planning isn't because we are lazy. In fact, when inspired, musicians and creative people can be really hard workers. As long as there is inspiration, we will go without eating or sleeping until that inspiration manifests itself into a creation. We don't struggle when inspiration is present and creativity is flowing, we struggle when the inspiration is absent. This is where the discipline must take over. This struggle exists in our personal walks with Christ as well. Spending time with God and communing with Him is important, not only when we feel like it, but when we don't as well. We are called to *pray without ceasing* (1 Thess. 5:17) and to be *steadfast, immovable, always abounding in the work of the Lord* (1 Cor. 15:58). These are disciplines that we learn. In the same way, we must discipline and train ourselves in the art of planning our worship sets.

Planning our sets

One of the keys to leading a smooth worship set starts with planning the set. There are several things to consider as we choose our songs. First, you never want to plan a set that your band can't execute. It is important for the worship leader to know the capabilities of the musicians who are serving on the team. An attitude of humility is so essential here. Years ago, I saw a football t-shirt that said, *"there is no I in team"* and this has to be our mentality as we lead our teams. Sometimes we are so excited about doing the hot new song that we neglect to think about how well our team will be able to play it. This is where we must ask ourselves: *What's more important, planning the new worship jam that just came out, or planning songs that our team can actually play well?* I would rather set my team up for success than taking a chance on failure. Understanding the demands of a song and your band's capabilities plays a huge role in maintaining excellence and consistency in your sets.

Secondly, every song should have a specific reason for being in the set. The job of the worship leader is to identify why a certain song needs to be sung at a certain time. A helpful philosophy that will prevent us from randomly choosing songs and randomly placing them in an order can be wrapped up in this saying: *Our songs are our sermons.* This has transformed the way I look at planning a set out. Much like the Pastor preaches his sermon, we are preaching through our songs and with our songs. Another way to look at it is that we are taking our congregation on a journey from the first song to the last and our job is to communicate that journey every step of the way. I call this *connecting the dots.* Our songs are the dots: the moments of corporate connection and response that center the people on a central theme. Connecting these dots means using the songs and the set as a platform to present the Gospel and not a curtain to hide behind. The congregation needs to be noticed and remembered as we start the journey of the set. So many times worship leaders just start their set and take off never looking back, leaving the congregation behind.

Lastly, the songs have to speak to us before we can lead them in speaking to our congregation. We have to be willing to pray over our songs and see how they lead us in worship first. If not, how can we lead our people to a place of worship that we have yet to go? We must also consider the demographics of our congregation and put their needs above our own desires when choosing songs. For instance, the "coolest" song might not always be the "best" song and we have to be okay with that. We are there to serve and minister to the people, even if that means planning songs that we don't really like.

One more important detail during the planning stage that often gets overlooked is the musical transitions from song to song. Good transitions keep people engaged while bad transitions encourage people to disengage. I view the worship set like a conversation. We want to be engaged with our listeners and we want to keep their attention so when we deliver those amazing truths of the Gospel, they don't miss it. Good transitions will keep the conversation going. They will keep the journey moving forward. And they will help our sets flow smoother. Remember, excellence is in the details.

Preparing

Planning is essential for setting the stage and preparing picks up where planning leaves off. After we have planned our set and taken time to worship to it ourselves, the next thing we need to focus on is preparing. This is another practice that takes discipline. The worship leader must take time and mentally walk through each song and map out the chords and the dynamics and decide on the arrangement and the key. We must make sure everyone has everything they need to show up and play. There should be clear objectives and roles for each musician and the worship leader brings it all together kind of like a conductor. This takes time, thought, and preparation. It is too easy to adopt a mindset of just throwing it all together; however, this is not honoring to God and giving our best to our congregations. This is not what God desires. God desires and expects our best; the first fruit of our gifts (Prov. 3:9), not just the left-overs.

Preparing our teams

Once we have a good idea of what we expect from our team, we must communicate with them. Some may need a one on one meeting to go over their parts. Some may just need a phone call to clear up any potential questions. Some may be able to take the charts and the arrangements that you have given them and be ready for rehearsal. Either way, we must know our team and prepare them accordingly. Having quality rehearsals that are efficient and effective will set the stage for everyone involved to be able to worship freely while they serve. Rehearsal should be just that… rehearsal. It should not be a place where everyone is listening to the songs and learning parts. I have been a part of very efficient rehearsals where everyone came prepared and things ran smoothly. I have also been a part of very inefficient rehearsals that seem to last forever without accomplishing anything. The former leaves the team feeling excited and ready to lead. The later leaves the team feeling defeated and not ready to lead.

Preparing our hearts

If we were to only focus on preparing our songs and teams each week, we would be missing the point of this entire book. As we have stated before, the most important instrument we bring to the stage is our heart and sadly, it is the instrument that is most often neglected. A friend of mine once said, *"You can always tell when a worship leader has been in the Word."* That statement struck me because it speaks of leading from the overflow of a heart that is filled and satisfied with God. It speaks of leading from a place of thankfulness and adoration. It speaks of leading from a place of brokenness and humility. And it speaks of how a worship leader's heart can impact a congregation. This is how worship should be. It should be contagious. It should be satisfying. It should be fulfilling. It should be exciting and joyful. It should be life changing and it all begins with preparing our hearts. When we are spending time during the week with God and meditating in His Word (Psalm 119:15-16), we are less likely to "go through the motions" and more likely to be consumed with gratefulness and thankfulness to Him (Psalm 100:4). We are more likely to make the most of every opportunity we have to serve Him and find delight in it. Some of the most impactful moments during worship happen when the worship leader shares what God has been teaching him through His Word. It is in these moments that worship is overflowing instead of being put on. It is in these moments that worship is real instead of being fake.

Hopefully, you have seen the benefits that come from preparing. When people know what is expected of them and what they are doing, serving is a joy instead of a burden and our worship team is more able to participate in worship instead of just facilitating it. Also, when we prepare our hearts, we are setting the stage for God to use us to lead His people in a mighty way.

Presence

Presence is something that many of us are uncomfortable talking about, however, it is one of those details that can have a dramatic effect on our leading. Presence is essentially our posture, or body language, while we are in front of others. Believe it or not, our presence can speak a louder message than the words that we say or the songs we sing. It reveals if we are joyful or burdened. It reveals if we are confident or insecure. It reveals if we are comfortable or uncomfortable. It reveals if we are engaged or unengaged. All this is communicated by our outward expressions and presence. Our job is to make sure our presence is singing the same song as our lips. This is where preparing our hearts is so important.

A Healthy Balance

If the hearts of the worship leaders aren't prepared and presence is at the center of too much focus, then our worship leading will not be genuine. It will be seen as shallow or put on. We will begin performing for the praise of the congregation instead of for the praise of God. I've been in some worship services where I felt as if the ones leading were trying way too hard. Their smiles seemed fake, their motions seemed rehearsed, and everything they did and said seemed exaggerated. I know that sounds super judgmental, but that is how I felt. It just didn't seem real and as a result, I couldn't allow myself to fully be lead by that team. However, to contrast that, if presence is not focused on at all, the verbal communication will begin to conflict with the non-verbal communication. For example, singing a chorus like, "*Oh happy day, you've washed my sin away*" with no joy, no excitement, no thankfulness on the face of the singer; just a big frown. It seems crazy, but I've seen it. As leaders and communicators, we have to be aware of this and seek to make sure all areas of expression are communicating the same message. Remember, we aren't performing for the praise of people and we shouldn't seek to entertain or impress them with our gifts (1 Thess. 2:6). Our gifts and our worship belong to the Lord (Ex. 20:3-5). The more a leader plans and prepares, the more comfortable and confident his/her presence will be.

There is a passage in Matthew 7:28-29 that speaks of the impact of Jesus' presence as He taught. It says, "*And when*

Jesus finished these sayings, the crowds were astonished at his teaching, for he was teaching them as one who had authority, and not as their scribes." He spoke with authority and that separated Him from the other teachers of the day. The crowds were astonished at what He was saying because of the *way* He said it. This speaks of the heart, mind, body, and soul all speaking the same message in perfect harmony (Mk 12:30). All of the parts making the same plea and working together to communicate the same message. This should be the case as we lead. Our excitement should be heard and also seen. Our joy should be told and also felt. Our love and adoration for God shouldn't just be empty words we sing, but rather, it should pour out from every part of our being. We should always be aware of what we are communicating, verbally and non-verbally, because we are reflections of Christ. Are we confident? Jesus is. Are we passionate? Jesus is. Are we filled with joy? Jesus is (Heb. 12:2). Are we truly happy that our sins have been washed away? Do we really believe that our God is greater than all? Are we really new creations in Christ? What message is our presence preaching? Our presence should always communicate the same message as our songs.

Breaking Through The Wall

Every week we stand before our congregations, there is an invisible wall that exists. It separates those on stage from those who are not. It keeps the congregation at a distance and identifies those on the platform as different. If we do not break through this wall, we will never be able to reach the people. We will never be able to connect with them. We will never be able to lead them. The first step in breaking through this wall is understanding what makes it up. The lights, the screens, the microphones, the podiums, the choir risers, and the pulpit or platform are all obstacles that can potentially create distance between us and our listeners. Our primary objective is to be seen as normal and attainable, not different and lofty. We want to have a conversation with our people so we must push these other things aside and connect with them. We need them to be participators and not mere spectators.

The most important and effective tool we have to break down this wall each week is communicating with our people. We have to be real. We have to be genuine. Truly and honestly putting our worship on display for the purpose of leading others is invaluable. However, it takes a person who is willing to be vulnerable for the sake of serving the church. This must be considered when adding people to the worship team. Our congregations are smarter than we think. They know when worship is being "put on" and when the people on stage are playing a role. They know when the vocalists would rather sing *at* them than *with* them. They aren't going to follow someone who seems confused or fake. We must break through the wall and establish common ground with our congregation and communicate that we are all in this together. We want them to join us. We need them to join us. We are a body unified by the blood of Christ and empowered by the Holy Spirit who becomes stronger when we are united together and not when we are separated.

Discussion

A) Discuss any moments of challenge, conviction, or encouragement during this week's reading.

B) Talk about the necessity of keeping the "heart" of worship before the "art" of worship. What are the potential problems in spending more time on the "art" than the "heart"?

C) Do you find it hard to plan out your teams and your sets in advance? Do you constantly have a problem with people showing up unprepared? Is excellence a standard that is consistently met in your ministry, or is it mediocrity? Discuss the relationship between the lack of planning and lack of performance. What are some practical ways you can become a better planner?

D) It is always important for leaders to prepare their teams as they lead. Jesus set this example for us as He constantly prepared His disciples for what lay before them. He knew what was to come and wanted them to be ready for it. One of the best examples is when He tells them of the trials and persecution they will face when He sends them out (Matt. 10:16-25) and as a result, they were faithful. In what ways are you preparing your teams to lead well? In what ways are you not preparing them? How are you helping them to prepare their hearts for worship each week?

E) What happens when you listen to a speaker who speaks monotone or with no excitement? How do you feel when you are watching someone who is extremely uncomfortable or nervous? What happens when you see someone who is sad? What happens when you see someone who is extremely excited? It is important for people to not only hear our hearts for worship, but see them as well. Read Psalm 95:1-6 and notice how there is a union between the content of the praises and the countenance of the response.

F) Talk about some practical ways you can "break through the wall" that separates you from the congregation and create an atmosphere of unity instead of division.

Take Away: The art is only as powerful as the heart is humble.

Summary

The most important instrument a worship leader has is his heart. If the enemy can corrupt or infect the heart of the worship leader, then he knows he can render him ineffective as a leader, and even worse, unacceptable as a worshiper. The sinfulness of our flesh and the selfishness of this world can fill our hearts and our minds with lies that will corrupt our understanding of our roles as worship leaders. Satan would want nothing more than to steal away God's worship by using misinformed and disillusioned worship leaders to place focus of God's people on the wrong things. We will eventually begin to make worship learning more about pleasing the people than God. It will become more about celebrating our greatness than His. Our motives will become selfish instead of selfless. Our worship will begin to shift from being only vertical to primarily horizontal. All of this can happen if we don't keep a close watch on the condition of our hearts.

One of the most devastating examples of this worship shift that we see in scripture is found in Genesis 11. After the flood, as people began to multiply on the earth, many found themselves settling in the land of Shinar. All the people spoke one language and they were growing in number and power. We see the worship shift take place in verse 4 when they desired to *"build a city and a tower with its tops in the heavens"* so they could *"make a name for themselves."* Their desire wasn't to please God. It was to please themselves. The people stopped being amazed by God and started being amazed by each other. Their hope, trust, and reliance shifted from being completely found in their Creator, to being found in their power. The creation began challenging the Creator for

His glory and praise. As a result, the Lord intervened and put in place barriers, such as language and distance, to protect the people from their own sinfulness (v.9).

In many ways, as we have discussed over the past several weeks, we are following in these same footsteps. Some of our worship leaders today want nothing more than to build the biggest tower they can. They do this by utilizing the gifts God has given them and the opportunities He has placed in front of them only to keep all the recognition and praise for themselves. This will most likely come natural to us as long as we are in the flesh. However, as we walk by the Spirit, our hearts want nothing more than to make Jesus the superstar, and not us. We must be proactive at fighting this battle because if we are not, we will lose. Walking by the Spirit is a discipline, but it is our only hope for conditioning our heart to love the Father more than ourselves (Gal. 5:16-17). Our churches are in desperate need of worship leaders whose heart's desire is to see the name of Christ lifted up in their congregations instead of their own.

Before moving on to the next section, **The Good Steward,** take a little time to read over Psalm 24:1-6 and examine your heart.

"The earth is the Lord's and the fullness thereof, the world and those who dwell therein, for he has founded it upon the seas and established it upon the rivers. Who shall ascend the hill of the Lord? And who shall stand in his holy place? He who has clean hands and a pure heart, who does not lift up his soul to what is false and does not swear deceitfully. He will receive blessing from the Lord and righteousness from the God of his

salvation. Such is the generation of those who seek him, who seek the face of the God of Jacob."

Meditation

A) Why are you leading worship? Is it to see generations seek the face of the Lord and dwell in His presence, or is it to gain a fan base for your talent?

B) What are the areas of your heart that wouldn't qualify as "pure"? What are the areas that you are "lifting up to another" instead of God?

C) What are the idols in your life that need to be confessed and forfeited for the sake of giving all of yourself to God?

Prayer Time

A) Pray that God would forgive you for chasing after and focusing on the wrong things as a worship leader.

B) Pray that through the power and conviction of the Holy Spirit, He will keep your "heart pure" and your "hands clean" as you progress as a worship leader.

C) Pray that by His power, all those under your care and leadership will draw closer to Him as He uses you to teach them and lead them into Christ exalting worship.

D) Pray also, that as the church worships in spirit and in truth, salvation will take place in the lives of the non-believers in our midst through the redeeming work of Christ and the power of the Holy Spirit.

Section 3
The Good steward

"The worship leader has to understand that just as our salvation is a gift of grace from God resulting from no works of our own; our opportunity to lead is a gift of grace as well."

The Good Steward

Being a good worship leader has everything to do with being a good steward. We talked in the last section about the misconceptions and misunderstandings our culture has about worship and worship leading. These misconceptions are a result of us taking the focus off of God and putting them on other things. We sometimes make worship leading more about the leader than the worship, more about the performance than the posture, and more about the fame than the Name. This happens when the focus shifts from the Creator to the created. The privilege becomes a right, the responsibility becomes a gig, and the joy eventually can become a burden. You see, when we are under the impression that our hard work and talents qualify us to lead, instead of the blood of Christ and God's grace, we become very proud and protective of our position. We want people to recognize our hard work and appreciate our abilities. We desire for people to think much of us and look up to us. We constantly feel that we have to prove ourselves to those around us in order to protect what is rightfully ours. The community of worship leaders can quickly begin to reek of competition instead of camaraderie, sizing up instead of building up, and division instead of unity. All of this is a result of not seeing our role as a steward. However, when we truly understand that everything we have has been given to us by a gracious and merciful God (1Cor. 4:7, James 1:17) and that we have done nothing to deserve the privilege of worshiping Him, much less leading worship, we begin to loosen the grip on what we thought was ours and begin to see things through the lenses of the steward.

Consider Your Calling

One of my favorite passages in the Bible is found in 1 Corinthians 1: 26-31. It is such a great reminder that our callings have nothing to do with us, but everything to do with God. He is not impressed with our strength, power, talents, or gifts because they are His to begin with. He isn't using us because He needs help in any way. Paul explains to us that God is interested in His glory, not ours. He wants His name to be exalted and known throughout the world, not ours. He will not share His glory or His praise with any other (Isaiah 42:8) for He is a jealous God (Ex. 34:14). This truth is so crucial for the worship leader. God will not share His glory with anyone, including us. The worship leader has to understand that just as our salvation is a gift of grace from God (Eph. 2:8) resulting from no works of our own, our opportunity to lead is a gift of grace as well. We have done nothing to deserve or earn it therefore, we should treat it with great care and do our best to be found trustworthy of receiving such a gift for this is the mark of a good steward (1 Cor. 4:2).

A trustworthy steward wants nothing more than to please the one to whom the gift belongs (Matt. 25:21). He desires to make the giver proud. He doesn't see the gift as a means of selfish gain, but selfless service (1 Peter 4:10). A trustworthy steward is motivated by gratitude and humility and mobilized by responsibility and obligation. Thankfulness fills his heart as love and appreciation guide his steps. He sees the incomparable value of the gift and is not satisfied until it has been completely exhausted and its greatest potential and impact has been maximized. Paul is one of the greatest examples of a trustworthy steward in scripture. He desired for the Gospel, and even his life to be maximized to its greatest potential for the sake of the glory of God (Philippians 1:20-21; 2:17). He saw every opportunity as a gift to use for the glory of God (1 Cor. 10:31). He also recognized that his privilege and position before God and man was a result of God's doing and not his own (Eph. 2:13, 1 Cor. 1:28-29). Worship leaders could learn a lot from Paul. He was one who had every right to put his confidence in the flesh and boast in his abilities (Philippians 3:4), but counted all his gain as loss because he was overwhelmed with the surpassing worth of knowing Christ (Philippians 3:7-8) and His forgiveness and redemption. Our worship leading should be centered on what Christ has done for us instead of what we can do for Him.

Other Good Stewards

Along with Paul, there are several other good stewards in scripture that we can learn from. All of these individuals were praised by Jesus for being trustworthy with what was given to them. The widow in Mark 12:41 brings to the Lord all that she has, though it was very little, while those around her were only giving a small portion of their abundance. Jesus praises her offering more than the others because she was concerned with blessing Him with all that she had more than anything else. Another example is found in Mark 14: 3-9. The woman at Bethany pours out her very expensive jar of perfume on Jesus' head even as the disciples are scolding her for not selling it for money. Jesus again praises her for using the best of what she had to worship Him. Finally, the first two servants in The Parable of the Talents in Matthew 25:14-30 also reveal to us the heart of a good steward. They took their talents and used them to their maximum potential resulting in the gifts being multiplied, while the other servant did nothing but protect and waste what was given to him. The first two servants saw the gifts as an opportunity to make their master proud, so they multiplied them. The other servant was so self-centered that his only focus and desire was not losing that which was given to him. Jesus praises the first two servants while He rebukes the last.

A Change in Perspective

Once we begin to see ourselves as stewards, our worship leading will become more about serving God and others, and less about serving ourselves. All the struggles with pride and ego seem to get buried by an attitude of appreciation and unworthiness. The temptation to fall back into the misconceptions and self-serving motives of worship leading that we talked about in the last section will become less desirable. Our goal will be to use our gifts to glorify Christ instead of using Christ to glorify our gifts. We will begin leading from a place of dependence instead of independence. Our greatest joy will not be found in being praised for our efforts, but in being found trustworthy as a steward (Romans 2:29).

Being a good worship leader has everything to do with being a good steward. Throughout these next several weeks we will look at how important it is for us to be faithful with all that has been given to us. We will focus on the responsibility we have to steward our calling, steward our gifts, steward our influence, and steward our impact. If we remain focused and faithful and honor God with all that has been entrusted to us, then our worship leading will be pleasing to Him and our impact for His Kingdom will be greater and reach further than we could ever imagine.

Week 10

The Call

"One thing we must understand is that a calling starts with God. He plans it and initiates it and therefore, gives us everything we need to carry it out."

The Call

To be called means to be singled out or set apart for a specific purpose by God. All of the great leaders in the Old Testament (Noah, Abraham, Isaac, Jacob, Joseph, Moses, Joshua, Nehemiah, David, Jeremiah, Isaiah, etc.) were called by God to be obedient and faithful in fulfilling the purposes He had set before them. Some had very small and specific callings while others had huge callings placed on their lives. Some were called to build, some were called to go, some were called to lead, some were called to fight, and some were called to speak. However, all were called to be obedient in carrying out the task laid before them. They were all hard workers, focused, and driven. They were visionary. They were revolutionary, standing out in the crowds rather than fitting in. Regardless of what the task was, these men have set a great example for us as to what it means to be trustworthy with our calling. They were who Paul was pointing us to when he said, *"walk in a manner worthy of the calling to which you have been called..."(Eph. 4:1).* They were steadfast and obedient in fulfilling their calling and the result was seeing God's people and God's plan advancing and His promises being fulfilled.

One thing we must understand is that a calling starts with God. He plans it and initiates it and therefore, gives us everything we need to carry it out. No one knew this better than Jeremiah. The Lord said to him in Jeremiah 1:5, *"Before I formed you in the womb I knew you, and before you were born I consecrated you; I appoint you a prophet to the nations."* Jeremiah was called out and set apart by God before he was born! God had planned and chosen for him to be His messenger to His people. God also provides Jeremiah with all that he will need to accomplish his task. *"Then the Lord put out His hand and touched my mouth. And the Lord said to me, 'Behold, I have put my words in your mouth. See, I have set you this day over nations and over kingdoms, to pluck up and to break down, to destroy and to overthrow, to build and to plant." (Jer. 1:9-10)* So, even in the midst of setbacks, obstacles, and rejection, we can be confident in our calling because we know it is through His strength and His power that we are moving and that what He started in us, He will complete (Philippians 1:6).

Just like Jeremiah, every believer has been called as well. We have been called out of darkness and into His marvelous light (1 Peter 2:9) so that we may be a holy nation and a people of God's own possession (James 1:18). He has set us apart to reflect Him to the world and every believer is responsible for doing just that. This is the general calling of the Church. For those of us called as worship leaders, we must never forget that this is what we are leading our people to do; to worship and reflect Jesus in their daily lives to the world around them. We have been entrusted with gifts and opportunities to help lead them in fulfilling their calling as believers. We must remember to be faithful in all circumstances and trust God to lead us like the men of faith in the Old Testament. Our hope and assurance must be found in Him and His purpose for our lives because there will be hard times that we encounter. It is during these times that we understand that our calling is more about a compulsion than convenience. We must be faithful stewards of what He has given us.

This week we will be discussing what it means to be a good steward of our calling, that reason or task for which we have been called out. If we are not being faithful with what little God has given us, then how can we expect Him to give us more (Matt. 25:21)? We will start off by talking, in more detail, about every believer's general calling and then we will discuss our specific callings.

General Calling

"But you are a chosen race, a royal priesthood, a holy nation, a people for his own possession, that you may proclaim the excellencies of him who called you out of darkness into his marvelous light."
1 Peter 2:9

All believers have a general calling to love God and worship Him with all of our heart, soul, mind, and strength (Mark 12:30) and to put none other before Him (Ex. 20:3). David describes this whole-hearted love and devotion towards God in Psalm 63 beautifully. He speaks of *earnestly* seeking after God. He describes his body and soul as *fainting* and *thirsting* for the Lord. This is our calling as believers. However, we get so distracted with the details of everyday life that many times, we are failing to steward this calling on our lives. We put work before Him. We put relationships before Him. We put worries and concerns before Him. We put money and security before Him. We even put fun before Him. This calling on the believer isn't optional. It is a commandment that we must obey.

Before any of us were born, God knew us. All the intricate parts of our being, He formed and put together (Psalm 139:13) and all of our days were numbered before any of them had ever begun (Psalm 139:16). We all have been "called out" of death and into the everlasting life that is found in Christ Jesus for the purpose of being Christ's witnesses (Acts 1:8) and His ambassadors to this world (2 Cor. 5:20). God is putting us on display and making His appeal through us for the lost to be reconciled to Himself. This is an amazing gift that not everyone is given, and He chose to give it to us. How are we stewarding this call? Do we love him with everything that we are and have? Do we put other things before Him? Do we reflect Him accurately to our friends? Do we point people to the redeeming work of Christ with our lives?

Along with the call to love and worship God only and be His witnesses, all believers are called to go and make disciples (Matt. 28:19) of all people. Going a step further than just being Jesus' witnesses, this commandment requires us to put ourselves in a position to lead someone else and shepherd their spiritual walk with the Lord. This is another great gift and responsibility that God is entrusting to us. He is asking us to represent Him, not only to the lost, but also to each other. We are to be His hands and feet, to teach about His ways and His character, to be the example to other believers the way Jesus was to His disciples. This means intentionally putting our lives on display, the victories and the defeats, for others to observe and grow from (1 Cor. 11:1). Before we worry about our specific calling, we need to make sure we are being faithful at fulfilling our general calling.

Specific Calling

"As each has received a gift, use it to serve one another, as good stewards of God's varied grace: whoever speaks, as one who speaks oracles of God; whoever serves, as one who serves by the strength that God supplies – in order that in everything God may be glorified through Jesus Christ." 1 Peter 4:10-11

Our specific calling is typically more related to the individual gifts we have been given. Where the general call is ongoing and eternal, the specific call can be seasonal and temporary. Where the general calling is universal, the specific calling is personal. Many times it is in our specific calling that we learn the most about God and His character because the tools He uses to communicate to us are so intimate and special to our heart. This is the beauty of God's grace. He gives us passions, desires, and gifts all for the purpose of revealing more of Himself to us so that we, in turn, can reveal more of Him to the world!

As we stated earlier, we are all called to worship God and be His reflection to the world by pointing everyone to Christ with our lives. However, each of us can accomplish this in different ways for there are a variety of gifts (1 Cor. 12:4), each given for the purpose of pointing people to Jesus. For

Noah, he built an ark (Gen. 6). For Moses, he led God's people out of slavery by parting the Red Sea (Ex. 14). For David, he defeated Goliath and lead God's people in victory over the Philistines (1 Sam. 17). For Job, he lost everything that he owned and loved for the sake of still worshiping God (Job 1:20-22). And Paul was sent to preach the message of reconciliation through Christ to the Gentiles (Acts 9:15). Each of these men's contribution to the Kingdom is equally important. One act isn't more special than the other. Each were faithful at carrying out their specific calling and using it to display God's glory. In the same way, we all have specific gifts that God has given to us for the sake of accomplishing the general call... glorifying Him to the world.

Some of us may be called specifically to a certain country to minister to a certain people-group much like Paul. Some of us may be called to minister in a particular occupation or career field. Others may be called to worship God and point people to Christ by caring for the homeless and less fortunate. Some of us may be called to use their talents such as music, art, dance, writing, photography, etc. as a way to spread the Gospel and minister to people. Some may be called to be parents, while others are called to be single. Some people have a love for big cities, while others prefer the wide-open spaces of the country. The point is that just as one body is made up of many different parts (1 Cor.12:12), there are many different ways that we, as believers, can accomplish our general calling through the specific gifts and passions that we have been given.

However, we must be careful not to abandon the general calling for the sake of the specific. There is an order to these two and being faithful and trustworthy to our general call should always precede our specific call. The fact is, you can't be a faithful steward with the specific without being faithful with the general. I believe this is what Jesus is referring to in Revelation 2:2-4 when He rebukes the church at Ephesus for forgetting their first love in the midst of all their good works and pursuits.

Discussion

A) Discuss any moments of challenge, conviction, or encouragement during this week's reading.

B) Think of a time when someone asked you to watch over something that belonged to them... their pet, their car, their house, their children, etc. It could be anything of value that they had temporarily entrusted you to watch over. How does your attitude change when you are responsible for someone else's property, and not just your own? The object becomes important to you not just because of its material worth, but more so, because of its worth in the eyes of its owner. How does this relate to our responsibility to lead God's people in worship of Him?

C) In Matthew 25: 29, we see that God is pleased and expects multiplication from the gifts that He gives. Not only is there a reward for those who do well with what they have been given, there is also punishment for those who do not do well with what they are given (v. 29-30). Discuss how this relates to you and your gifts.

D) The word "calling" can mean many different things for many different people. The best practical description I have heard regarding a calling is: *"You know you are called to do something when you can't not do it."* What does this mean? Should a calling placed on us by God ever be stopped or hindered by the obstacles brought on by man?

E) Remember the phrase: *"We must be worshipers before we are worship leaders"?* Well we, as worship leaders, are saying the exact same thing when we say we must fulfill our general calling before we fulfill our specific calling. We can't be faithful stewards of our music and influence if we aren't being faithful in worshiping God with all that we are and using all that we have to point people to Jesus. Talk about how keeping this mindset will affect your worship leading.

F) There is a difference in loving worship and loving music, and being called to lead worship. When God calls a person to do something, He equips them with the gifts and tools they will need to accomplish the task. Do you have the tools necessary to steward this calling well? Would others agree with you? There should be fruit and growth in the life and ministry of someone walking out their calling. Evaluate your calling. Do you love music and worship, or is leading worship something that you HAVE to do? Do you make excuses for not excelling or giving your best? What fruit do you see in your ministry?

Take Away: We must be faithful with our general calling before we can be effective with our specific calling.

Week 11

The gift

"Whether spiritual or physical, every gift finds it's origin in the Father. He is our Provider and without Him, we would have nothing."

The Gift

If you have ever observed a house being built, then you know that it is a very complicated task. There are many different tools and pieces of equipment needed to accomplish each stage of this process. Bulldozers are used to clear the land and cement trucks are used to pour the foundation. Gas and oil is needed to enable these vehicles to run and do their job properly. Lumber, hammers, and nails are used to frame up the structure of the house while all sorts of pipes and shovels are used for the plumbing. All kinds of wiring and conduit are run throughout the house for electricity. Sheet rock is needed to hang on the interior of the house while siding or brick is placed on the exterior. Tar paper and shingles are placed on the roof with special roofing nails while flooring, cabinetry, and crown molding are installed on the inside with specialized nail guns. Paint rollers and brushes are used to paint the walls while insulation is blown or tacked in between them. Finally, doors, windows, and appliances are set in place as the home is now complete.

Out of all the tools used to build the home, none will ever get the attention and recognition that the completed home gets. People will appreciate and admire the beauty of the finished work, not the tools that were used to build it. You see, tools aren't meant to be the focus of attention and appreciation. They are meant to serve something greater. Their only purpose is to perform their specific task well. When all tools work together properly, the end result is a beautiful creation that can now fulfill its purpose. Tools and instruments should always point to something greater than themselves much like a musical instrument points not to itself, but to the music it creates. We are tools God is using to build His kingdom (1 Peter 2:5) and all the gifts, talents, and abilities He has given us are nothing more than tools as well. They were not given to us for any other reason than to point to His greatness and His beauty.

Every gift comes from God (James 1:17) and many times these gifts are the very instruments or tools we need to carry out the calling that has been placed on our lives. Whether spiritual or physical, every gift finds its origin in the Father. He is our Provider and without Him, we would have nothing (Psalm 23:1). He chooses to give certain gifts to certain people for the purpose of accomplishing certain tasks, much like the tools used to build the house. Everyone can't have the same gift just like every tool can't be a hammer. Only when the variety of gifts are working together is the body of Christ functioning properly and most effectively (1 Cor. 12:14). To some He gives wisdom and others He gives compassion. To some He gives the gift of prophecy and others, the gift of evangelism. To some He gives the gift of teaching and to others He gives the gift of shepherding (Eph. 4:11). To some He gives the gift of music and art while others He gives the gift of discernment. However, all these gifts are given for the same purpose of pointing to Christ and exalting the Father through the Holy Spirit (1 Cor. 12:4) and building up the church for the work of sharing Christ with the world (Eph. 4:12).

In order to be good stewards of our gifts, we must see them as tools and stop seeing them as something that we have earned or achieved. Many of us don't treat our gifts like gifts at all; rather we treat them like our property. We don't see them as things entrusted to us or given to us, but things that were earned by us. Therefore, it is hard for us not to exalt our gifts at times, and begin taking from God the worship that is rightfully His. However, we cannot ignore our gifts either. They are given to us for a reason and for the purpose of being used up. They are important enough to God for Him to give them to us, so we must be good stewards and treat them with great importance. This can be a slippery slope for the worship leader because he must see his gift as important, but not more important than the One who gave it to him. This is a tight rope that we must continually walk but remembering that our gifts are mere tools that were given to us by God for His exaltation and His purposes, will keep us balanced. Here are some other gifts of great worth and importance that sometimes get overlooked.

The Gift of Jesus

"for all have sinned and fall short of the glory of God, and are justified by his grace as a gift, through the redemption that is

in Christ Jesus, whom God put forward as a propitiation by his blood, to be received by faith." Romans 3: 23-25

Jesus is the most important gift of all! Without Him, there is no salvation, redemption, and restoration for man. We would be eternally separated from God by the chasm created by our sin. Jesus is the one who stands in the gap between God and man as our Mediator and for believers, imputing His righteousness to us so that we are seen as acceptable before a Holy God (2 Cor. 5:21). He has paid our debt and purchased our pardon completely. His work will never weaken or run out. Death has been defeated and the enemy will one day be eternally destroyed when Jesus comes back to rescue His bride, the Church (Eph. 5:25-27, Rev. 19:7-9). This is why it is so important that Jesus is appreciated and acknowledged in our worship times. He should always be the center of our attention and affection because apart from Him, we cannot worship.

The Gift of the Holy Spirit

"When the Spirit of truth comes, he will guide you into all the truth, for he will not speak on his own authority, but whatever he hears he will speak, and he will declare to you the things that are to come." John 16:13

When Jesus was preparing to leave this earth, He communicated that He would not leave us alone (John 14:18). He would send us a "Helper" to lead us in the same way that He led the disciples during His earthly ministry. The Holy Spirit is that helper who teaches us and guides us into a deeper knowledge and awareness of God's character and nature (John 14:26). He will also convict the world concerning sin, righteousness, and judgment (John 16:8). For the believer, the Holy Spirit dwells within us forever (John 14:17) and empowers us to be a witness for Christ and spread the Gospel to the ends of the earth (Acts 2:8). It is incredibly important that the Holy Spirit has room to move and work in our corporate worship times, for without Him, we can very easily get lost. He is the one who is illuminating God to us and guiding us into His presence in spirit and truth, so why aren't we looking to Him more? Question to think about: If the Holy Spirit didn't show up in your service this week, would you know the difference?

The Gift of God's Word

"Until I come, devote yourself to the public reading of Scripture, to exhortation, to teaching. Do not neglect the gift you have, which was given you by prophecy when the council of elders laid their hands on you." 1 Timothy 4:13-14

God's word is His direct revelation of Himself. J.I. Packer states, *"nobody would know the truth about God, or be able to relate to Him in a personal way, had not God first acted to make Himself known."* [18] We would continue to be lost and helpless if He hadn't given us this gift to teach us about salvation. His word is His voice to us. It is the only absolute truth there is (John 17:17) in a world in desperate need of it. It is through the lens of God's word that we learn about Him, us, and eternity and it is only through the power of the Holy Spirit that this truth awakens our souls and raises us to new life.

God's word is living and active (Heb. 4:12) meaning it is still relevant to our culture, our problems, and our fears today and therefore, is a vital source of teaching, correcting, and equipping (2 Tim. 3:16) for the people in our churches. They need it and it is our job to give it to them as we work to present all blameless and mature in Christ (Col. 1:28). Worship leaders must see the importance of utilizing God's word into their worship sets. It is what gives our songs their credibility. If we are seeking to worship "in spirit and in truth" and His word is "living and active", then we should be implementing scripture into our times of worship.

The Gift of Time

"Behold, you have made my days a few handbreaths, and my lifetime is as nothing before you. Surely all mankind stands as a mere breath!" Psalm 39:5

Out of all the gifts that we are given, this one is wasted the most! One of the greatest weapons the enemy can use against us is the expectation that we have tomorrow. Just think of all the conversations we are putting off right now because we think we have time to do it later. Just think of the impact we could be having for the Gospel right now that is absent because we are waiting on all the circumstances to be perfect. God has a purpose and a plan for everything that He creates (Rev. 4:11) and only He knows when that purpose has been fulfilled. We haven't been called to rewrite God's plan, or even approve it. We have been called to be obedient to Him and to be good stewards of the gifts He decides to give us. Every day, every moment, and every breath is a gift from God.

He intimately knew us, even before we were created, and had all our days numbered before the first one ever began (Psalm 139:15-16). Our time is limited and we should be making the most of it.

The Gift of Music

"Praise the Lord! For it is good to sing praises to our God; for it is pleasant, and a song of praise is fitting." Psalm 147:1

Music has always played an important role in God's story because music is important to God. God delights in His people (Psalm 149:4) and draws near to us as we praise and worship Him (Psalm 22:3). He not only desires us to sing to Him, but He rejoices over us with singing (Zeph. 3:17). Music and singing is also a common occurrence in heaven with the angels (Isaiah 6:2-3, Rev. 4:6-8). It has also served as an effective tool in leading God's people since the beginning. We see Moses and the Israelites break into song after the Egyptians were defeated at the Red Sea (Ex. 15). We see Solomon and the people singing and making music as they brought the ark to the Temple (2 Chron. 5:13) and then, we see God's approval of their worship as His glory appears (2 Chron. 5:14). Psalms is full of songs written by true worshipers such as David, as they express their love, devotion, and dependence on God throughout every season of life. Jesus also leads His disciples in song as He is teaching and preparing them for what is to come (Mark 14:26).

Music still plays a vital role in leading and communicating to God's people today. When the worship leader truly understands how to use it and the impact that it can have, the results can be powerful. Music has a way of reaching down into the depths of our souls and speaking a language that none other can speak. A language that communicates not only to our minds and our intellect, but also to our hearts and our emotions. It can pull out feelings that we never knew existed. It can be very instrumental in shaping our attitudes and our desires. Music can prompt a response, or music can be the response. As worship leaders, we must understand why we sing and how music affects us if we are going to use this tool effectively when leading. Here are some biblical reasons why we sing.

1) We sing to praise God and exalt His name above all others. (Psalm 7:17, Psalm 9:2, Psalm 66:2)

2) We sing to celebrate salvation. (2 Sam. 22:1-4, Psalm 98)

3) We sing to draw near to God. (Psalm 22:3, Psalm 100:4)

4) We sing in response to God and His works. (Psalm 95:1, Psalm 101:1, Psalm 150)

5) We sing to remind ourselves of His faithfulness and power. (Psalm 59:16-17, Psalm 71:22, 1 Chron. 16:23)

6) We sing to testify to His great work in our lives. (Ex. 15:1, Psalm 40:3, Romans 15:9)

7) We sing to minister to others. (1 Sam. 16:23, 1 Cor. 14:15)

8) We sing to encourage other believers. (Heb. 2:12, Col. 3:16)

Discussion

A) Discuss any moments of challenge, conviction, or encouragement during this week's reading.

B) As good stewards of our gifts, we must understand the importance of seeing the value of our gift without placing it above God. We know that we can't make it an idol, but we also know from Matt. 25: 14-30 that we must value it and use it to share Christ with the world. Do you see your gifts and abilities as important tools to take the Gospel to your community, city, and even the world? In what ways are you utilizing your gifts well? In what ways are you wasting your gifts?

C) Many times in planning and preparing our services each week, we spend all of our time focusing on all the logistics such as songs, transitions, announcements, the message, baptisms, new members, etc. It is very easy to roll into a Sunday morning without taking time to ask the Holy Spirit to lead and guide you as you lead. Discuss that question from earlier: If the Holy Spirit didn't show up this week in your service, would you know the difference?

D) Read Ecclesiastes 3:1-8. What do these verses do to your perspective on life? Do you see your life, your gifts, and your influence as a passing season? How does seeing them this way change the way you use them?

E) When David was assembling the musicians and appointing the Levites to carry out the tasks of ministering before the ark of the Lord with music and singing in 1 Chronicles 15, he assigns Chenaniah as the director in verse 22. His reasoning for placing him in charge of all the music was because *"he understood it."* It is one thing to know how to play music, but it is another thing to understand how music works and communicates. Do you understand music or do you just know how to play it? Think of ways you can improve on understanding how music communicates more and how you can become a better director of music for your band.

Take Away: Always use your gifts to glorify Christ and never use Christ to glorify your gifts.

Week 12

The influence

"Influence is a powerful gift that should be treated with great respect. If used appropriately, it can be the greatest weapon for the advancement of the Gospel. If used inappropriately, it can be the greatest hindrance."

The Influence

Just like the gifts we talked about last week, the ability and opportunity to influence people for the sake of the Gospel is an amazing gift as well. God calls out, gives gifts, and places people in positions of leadership so that His plan and His purposes will be fulfilled. Influence can be used as a powerful tool for the Gospel. It motivates and mobilizes people. It changes people and moves them from one way of thinking to another. It can shift attitudes and alter perspectives. It can make people see something that they didn't see before. Influence is the greatest tool a leader can have because without it, he can't lead. If Moses never influenced the Israelites, they would have never been set free and witnessed God do incredible miracles in their midst. If Joshua never influenced God's people, they would have never crossed the Jordan and seen the walls of Jericho come crashing down. If Peter never had influence over the masses, thousands would have never responded to the Gospel of Jesus (Acts 2:41). If Jesus had never influenced 12 disciples, the Church would not exist today. Just to be clear, it is the power of God alone that accomplishes the impossible and brings the dead to life. Our influence is only a tool that He chooses to use for His purposes and we are stewards of that influence. *"And I, when I came to you, brothers, did not come proclaiming to you the testimony of God with lofty speech or wisdom. For I decided to know nothing among you except Jesus Christ and him crucified. And I was with you in weakness and in fear and much trembling, and my speech and my message were not in plausible words of wisdom, but in demonstration of the Spirit and of power, so that your faith might not rest in the wisdom of men but in the power of God." 1 Corinthians 2:1-5*

We are Instruments of Influence

Many times God chooses to exalt a man and use him to influence His people for the sake of exalting Himself. He gives him power and He gives him influence for the sake of getting His glory. This is revealed in God's conversation with Joshua as He is preparing him to lead the people across the Jordan River. He says in Joshua 3:7, *"Today I will begin to exalt you in the sight of all Israel, that they may know that, as I was with Moses, so I will be with you."* Influence is about trust. God made Joshua trustworthy in the sight of the people by committing several miracles under his leadership. This earned the people's trust in Joshua. They saw his courage and trusted that he was listening to God. As a result, God's people followed Joshua into the Promised Land and got to experience the faithfulness and rest of the Lord.

So, how are we being good stewards of our influence? Are we using it to lead our people to a greater appreciation and dependency on Christ, or are we using it to gain a greater fan base? Do our people follow us because they trust that God is with us, or because they are impressed by our gifts? Are we using our influence to point them towards Jesus, or ourselves? We must remember that God didn't choose us because of our abilities. Many times, He chooses leaders for their inabilities because it is in their inabilities that His ability shines (Eph. 3:20). He doesn't always choose the strongest, richest, best looking, most talented, or most popular. Most of the time He chooses the exact opposite. He calls the weakest (David), the lowest (Jesus), and the least liked (Saul/Paul) to shame the strong and wise all so that no human may boast in the presence of the Lord (1 Cor. 1:28-29). Influence is a powerful gift that should be treated with great respect. If used appropriately, it can be the greatest weapon for the advancement of the Gospel. If used inappropriately, it can be the greatest hindrance.

Jesus was the greatest influencer this world has ever known. His message and His impact are still advancing today to every nation and every tongue. In the 3 years of His ministry on earth, Jesus maximized every gift, moment, and opportunity as a communicator. He realized the great power of influence and He used it well. Before we go any further in discussing the practical aspects of influencing people, we must understand that the greatest influencer is the Holy Spirit (John 14:25-26) and we can do nothing of eternal value apart from Him. He is the greatest influencer and our main priority should be to be used by Him. There are, however, some practical things that we should have if we want to be good stewards of the influence given to us. This week we are going to look at the importance of having vision and clarity.

Vision

"Where there is no vision, the people perish." Proverbs 29:18

Apart from the Holy Spirit, vision is the most important ingredient when influencing people. Vision has the ability to look at the impossible and see the possible. It has the ability to look into the darkness and see light. Vision has to ability to see life in the midst of death. A great example of this comes when Jesus looks at Lazarus and instead of seeing a dead man He sees the potential for life and influence (John 11:4). Vision sees not only the seen, but the unseen as well. It brings hope and clarity to a world in desperate need of it. We stated in the first section that man is left wandering around in a state of confusion and spiritual death because sin has separated him from his created purpose. Where there was no way, God made a way (John 3:16) through His son Jesus (Romans 8:1-2). Now, because of God's grace and His purpose and will, or His vision, we have the most amazing message of hope in the world. We have the Gospel. However, we must realize that there is a consequence for no vision according to Proverbs 29:18 and this consequence is death.

It is important for us as worship leaders to have vision as we lead. Having a clear understanding of what we are doing and why we are doing it will help us be more effective influencers of Christ-centered worship. We have to constantly be seeking and listening to the Lord's direction for our ministry. Much of our direction should come from our Lead Pastor's vision for the church. If He is seeking the Lord for direction like Moses, Joshua, and Jesus, then he should have vision. Every ministry in the church exists to fulfill the vision of the church and the worship ministry is no different. It is within this vision for the church that we, worship leaders, develop our vision; for we should always be striving for alignment and unity as we serve and lead. Here is an example of our worship team's vision statement. Notice how each line is intentional and vision filled. This serves as a statement to teach about who we are and why we do what we do, but it also serves as a tool to keep us on track if we start loosing focus. So in this case, vision not only directs, but vision also corrects!

Vision Statement:

"We are dedicated followers of Christ who use our gifts as nothing more than a tool to focus the hearts of our listeners on God, teach them about His character, and deliver the life changing message of the Gospel."

The Break down

"We are dedicated followers of Christ..."

This is stated first because it is the most important. People should see our love for Jesus and His love and light in our lives not just on stage, but always. We are worshipers before we are worship leaders. If we don't have this in order, chances are we are leading people to worship something other than Christ. *"Woe to the shepherds who destroy and scatter the sheep of my pasture!" declares the Lord. (Jer. 23:1)*

"who use our gifts..."

The foundation of our ministry, like the foundation of the Gospel, is about serving and not being served (Phil. 2:5-8). We exist to minister to the people with our gifts and sometimes that means choosing songs we wouldn't normally choose for the sake of shepherding our flock better. We have to put the needs of our people above our own personal preferences. Our gifts were given to us to advance God's kingdom and not our own. *"What do you have that you did not receive? If then you received it, why do you boast as if you did not receive it?" (1 Cor. 4:7)*

"as nothing more than a tool..."

We have to understand that we are just a very small part of a much bigger picture. Just like a hammer is a small, but vital, part in constructing a house; our gifts play a small part in God's great plan of redeeming humanity for the sake of His glory. In the same way a hammer can be replaced if it stops being useful to building the house, we can be replaced if our gifts stop becoming tools and start becoming idols. God doesn't need our gifts, He wants our hearts. *"Who shall ascend the hill of the Lord? And who shall stand in His holy place? He who has clean hands and a pure heart, who does not lift up his soul to what is false and does not swear deceitfully."(Psalm 24:3-4)*

"to focus the hearts of our listeners on God..."

The truth is that people are walking into our services every week thinking about everything else but God and worshiping Him with all their heart, soul, mind, and strength. Some are carrying burdens that we could never imagine such as the death of a loved one, a terminal illness, depression and hopelessness, thoughts of suicide, divorce, adultery, etc. These are battles that we must face head on each week with our efforts. We should strive to take our congregation's mind off of their afflictions and put it on the greatness of our God who has overcome (John 16:33) because we know that those who look to Him are radiant and will never be put to shame (Ps. 34:5). *"For we do not wrestle against flesh and blood, but against the rulers, against the authorities, against the cosmic powers over this present darkness, against the spiritual forces of evil in the heavenly places." (Eph. 6:12)*

"teach them about His character..."

We have to be clear that our gifts and our efforts are not meant for the entertainment and praise of man. Not only do we speak to people's emotions with our music and various forms of production, but we also speak to their minds and intellect through teaching. Therefore, we must be familiar with God's word and assume the mindset that *"our songs are our sermons."* We must be intentional about using moments in our sets to present the truth of God's word so we can help equip our congregations to stand strong in their faith in our world that is trying to break them down. *"For the time is coming when people will not endure sound teaching, but having itching ears they will accumulate for themselves teachers to suit their own passions, and will turn away from listening to the truth and wander off into myths." (2 Tim. 4:3-4)*

"and deliver the life changing message of the Gospel."

We have the most important message to communicate each week, a message of hope, purpose, redemption, and eternity. This message is the Gospel and the people in our communities are in desperate need of it. Therefore, we have to make sure that Jesus is central in everything we do and say and that the presentation of the Gospel is clear and free from all distractions. This can be difficult when using many different forms of media and technology. If we are going to use these things, let's use them to help communicate the Gospel more clearly and more effectively, and not allow them to get in the way. This takes prayer, practice, and preparation. This also means that some people may not be the best choice to put on stage to lead in music. We cannot forget that we are communicating as we lead and when there are distractions after distractions, it becomes hard to communicate effectively. The presentation of the Gospel is king over everything else. *"For you remember, brothers, our labor and toil: we worked night and day, that we might not be a burden to any of you, while we proclaimed to you the gospel of God." (1 Thess. 2:9)*

Clarity

"For God is not a God of confusion, but of peace." 1 Corinthians 14:33

Having vision is one thing, but being able to communicate it clearly to influence others is another. This is an extremely difficult task that Jesus even had a hard time with. Throughout His ministry, He was constantly communicating and casting vision about Himself and His ministry and His disciples still didn't get it all the time. As we are leading our teams, we have to be clear in communicating our vision if we want unity and commitment. We have to be as intentional about teaching our musicians what it means to worship and serve, as we are about using them to pull off a worship set. We cannot forget that we are their shepherds too and we have a responsibility to pour into their lives and minister to them outside of the music. When there are questions left unanswered, there is the possibility for confusion and misunderstandings, and most all problems result from confusion or misunderstandings. Clarity is the most important tool a worship leader can have as he begins to build his ministry. It will ensure that the heart of the worship leader and his vision doesn't get lost as his ministry and influence expands. Here are three things to keep in mind as we build our ministry.

Communicate

As we begin building our ministries, communication is vital to growth and clarity. Every chance we get we need to be communicating the vision to our team. We are going to have many people with different influences and expectations joining our ministries, and communication is the key to keeping everyone on the same page. These people will be looking to us for vision, direction, and guidance and the only way to give it to them is to communicate. Jesus was always communicating to His disciples. He used prayer to communicate and teach them (Matt. 6:9-13). He communicated to them as He taught the masses (Matt. 5). He used parables and miracles (Matt. 15:32-39) for communicating vision. He used moments of uncertainty and fear (Matt. 14:22-32) as well as moments of rebuke (Matt. 12:25-34) to continue to cast vision about who He was. If Jesus had to be this intentional about communication, then how much more do we? Too much communication is good communication.

Delegate

If there was ever a person who didn't need to delegate, it was Jesus. He was completely capable in Himself to handle anything He needed to accomplish. However, much like in baptism, He chose to do it in order to set the example for us. Jesus sought out disciples to invest in and train as soon as His ministry began (Matt. 4:18). In the same way, we must seek people that will come alongside us and help carry the weight so we can continue to focus on casting vision and continuing clarity for our team. If we are so busy doing things that others can be doing, we are neglecting our responsibilities as a believer and as a leader. Our call as believers is to "*make disciples*"(Matt. 28:19) and our call as leaders is to *"equip the saints to do the work of the ministry"* (Eph. 4:12). As we build our ministry and the workload increases, our job isn't to do all the work. Our job is to equip others in order to multiply our influence, just like Jesus did.

Evaluate

In striving for clarity as we communicate, evaluation is necessary. Without evaluation, our teams won't know the wins from the losses. They won't know what is good from what is bad. Without evaluation, all of our teachings, directions, and standards are in vain because there is no enforcement. Evaluation is the enforcement and people want to be evaluated so they know if they are performing well. Evaluation was important to Jesus. We see Him constantly evaluating His disciples with gentle rebukes (Matt. 14:31), hard rebukes (Mark 8:33), tough questioning (Matt. 16:15), and affirming praises (Matt. 16:17). Jesus even sends us the Holy Spirit to dwell within us and to convict and correct us when we get off track (John 16:13). If we are being sanctified, then shouldn't our ministries? We can say all day long that rehearsal starts at 5:00 p.m., but if we continue to allow it to start at 5:30 p.m., then that standard means nothing. Evaluation is needed to enforce our standards. We must remember to reflect Christ and the fruit of the Spirit as we are evaluating our teams (Gal. 5:22-23).

Discussion

1) Discuss any moments of challenge, conviction, or encouragement during this week's reading.

2) Are you being a good steward of the influence that God has given you? We must never forget the words God spoke to Joshua, *"Today I will begin to exalt you in the sight of all Israel, that they may know that, as I was with Moses, so I will be with you." (Joshua 3:7).* He gives us influence so that people will see Him in us and He will be glorified as we lead. Discuss if and how you are glorifying God with your influence.

3) Take some time to think about the vision, heartbeat, personality, and identity of your church. Now, pair that with the vision that God has given you for the worship ministry in the context of your church and people. Write out a vision statement much like the one in the reading that keeps the vision and purpose in the minds and hearts of your team members. It should answer the questions: Who are we? What are we doing? Why are we doing it?

4) We have talked about the benefits of communicating vision clearly with our team and how it keeps everyone motivated and on the same page. We also know from Proverbs 29:18, that vision is not merely a suggestion. It is necessary for sustaining life and purpose and without it there is confusion, chaos, and death. Discuss the consequences of not having vision or not

communicating vision clearly that you have seen in your ministry and possible solutions that could fix it.

5) Read 1 Timothy 3:1-2. In regards to being a good steward of the influence God has given us, do you strive to live a life that is above "reproach", or blame? 2 Peter 3:14 says, *"make every effort to be found living peaceful lives that are pure and blameless in His sight."* Are you willing to make "every effort", or just the ones that are convenient and easy? Read 1 Corinthians 10:31 and discuss.

Take Away: Influence isn't an instrument of power meant for our benefit, but a burden of responsibility meant to exalt Jesus and His redeeming work! We should handle it with the utmost care and respect.

Week 13

The impact

"The harsh reality is that our moment of influence will pass, but our impact doesn't have to. In fact, our impact should carry on if we are following Jesus' example."

The Impact

While influence is more localized and touches those who are near to us, impact is more widespread and far reaching, much like the "ripple effect". When a rock is thrown into a lake, the initial splash from the rock hitting the water is the influence. The rock is influencing the current state of the surface of the water when it strikes it. What happens next is the impact. Waves or ripples begin expanding outward from the initial point of contact carrying the influence further out. What started with a small localized influence resulted in an impact that effects half the lake. This very same concept applies as we lead. If we are truly good stewards of our influence and lead with clarity and vision; it is possible for our influence to reach much further and stick around much longer than we do. It is possible for our influence to not only impact our generation, but our children's and grandchildren's generation. Who's to say it has to stop there? We are not only working for the moment, but we are working for the future.

We are striving to lead not only our church's current congregation into a more intimate life of worship with God, but future congregations as well. Isn't that a humbling thought? Our impact could be reaching, teaching, inspiring, and equipping generations for the Gospel long after we are gone.

Building an Impactful Ministry

We have to be *intentional* about building a ministry that will carry on in our absence, one that will carry the influence of the Gospel to other generations. We must find a way to get beyond ourselves and know that the Gospel and the worship of God's people are much bigger than we are. For many worship leaders, including myself, this can be hard. We seem to think that we are the experts in worship at times, (or at least I do), and this can cause us to exalt ourselves to a position we do not need to be in. We can begin to see ourselves as indispensable. The truth is that God, His plan, His people, His worship, and His kingdom existed before us and will continue on long after we are gone. We are merely small tools that are being used, at this particular moment in time, to build up God's kingdom and lead His people into a greater appreciation of Him with our gifts. Are we striving to build a ministry that will outlast us? Are we building up and preparing others to take over when we step aside? The harsh reality is that our moment of influence will pass, but our impact doesn't have to. In fact, our impact should carry on if we are following Jesus' example.

We know that Jesus came in obedience to the Father to satisfy God's wrath on mankind's sin by dying on the cross, but do we ever see Jesus as a ministry builder? He not only came to die for our sins, but He also came to begin His ministry, His kingdom, and His church here on earth. He did it well because the impact of His influence is still being felt today and His church is continuing to grow and advance over 2000 years later. He was a good steward of His gifts and influence and He saw the importance of calling out and equipping others to lead (Matt. 4:19). He taught them. He spent time with them. He challenged them. He empowered them. He tested them. He corrected them. He led them. Finally, He sent them out to imitate Him and be an ambassador for Him (Matt. 28:19-20, 2 Cor. 5:20) to the world. He had equipped them with everything they would need, including the Holy Spirit, to carry on after Him and we must strive to do the same. "*Making disciples*" isn't a suggestion, but rather, a command and therefore, must be a priority in our ministry.

We can't be so focused on the details of our sets and the production of our services that we neglect the potential disciples around us whom God may want us to raise up and send out. We must put others in the spotlight and give them opportunity to shine, and even fail. Sometimes the greatest lessons are learned from failing and making mistakes. Jesus allowed His disciples to fail many times throughout His ministry (Matt. 14:31, Matt. 26:36-46, Matt. 26:75), all for the purpose of equipping them to take it over. Just think, if Jesus did not raise up disciples and send them out, would we know the Gospel today? We are still experiencing the ripple effects of Jesus' ministry, and even more, we are products of it!

As I have studied Jesus and how He built His ministry, there are three characteristics that I have noticed being woven in and out of everything He did. These characteristics can teach us a lot about being effective at influencing people and

leaving a lasting impact for the Gospel. Following Jesus
means much more than just listening to what He said; it means
doing what He did (Matt. 16:24). As worshipers, we must live
the way He lived and worship the way He worshiped. As
worship leaders, we must lead the way He led and influence
the way He influenced. I seek to imitate Jesus in my personal
life, but I also seek to imitate Him in my life as a leader. I
want to serve like He served and give like He gave. I want to
teach like He taught and train like He trained. I want to equip
like He equipped and impact like He impacted. If our
ministries are going to influence and impact those around us
like Jesus did, these three characteristics must be present in
everything we do: 1) Give 2) Grow 3) Go.

Give

*"Even as the Son of Man came not to be served but to serve,
and to give his life as a ransom for many." (Matt. 20:28)*

Jesus came and set the perfect example of what it means to
serve, and that same heart should be reflected in our ministry.
He was God in flesh (Col. 2:9) and yet He still made Himself
nothing and came to this earth ultimately to serve (Philippians
2:6-8), even to the point of death. This idea of the powerful
One being poured out and the exalted One being made low is
in stark contrast to our culture today. We have to be very
careful as worship leaders not to be influenced by our culture
and build a ministry that breeds entitlement more than self-
sacrifice, or competition more than encouragement. It is not
enough for us to just "look like Christ", we must "be like
Christ" and have His heart even in the deepest parts of our

lives and ministries. Though Jesus is divine, He became nothing. Though He is the King of Kings, He came as a servant. Though He is supreme over all, He came in humility. Though He is infinite, He put on the limitations of a physical body all for the sake of glorifying His Father through providing reconciliation for us through His blood (Romans 5:10). We must follow in Jesus' footsteps here and be servant leaders, not leading from a place of entitlement and arrogance, but a place of brokenness and humility (2 Peter 5:2-3). We are servants and not rock stars. We are shepherds and not kings. Shepherds exist to serve the flock, the flock doesn't exist to serve the shepherd!

Serve God

"For I have come down from heaven, not to do my own will but the will of him who sent me." John 6:38

Our call as believers is to love God and serve Him in everything we do (Luke 10:27), individually and corporately, as the body of Christ. Jesus' desire to serve His Father fueled everything He said and did from coming to the earth, to ministering to and teaching people, to calling and equipping His disciples, and ultimately to dying on the cross. In the same way we, as worship leaders, have to understand that we are called to be faithful servants of God before anything or anyone else. There are many false idols out there competing aggressively for our worship, however these are nothing more than broken cisterns that will never satisfy (Jer. 2:13). We were not made to serve lesser gods, but rather, the one true God through Jesus Christ.

Serve each other

"Put on then, as God's chosen ones, holy and beloved, compassionate hearts, kindness, humility, meekness, and patience, bearing with one another and, if one has a complaint against another, forgiving each other; as the Lord has forgiven you, so you must also forgive." Colossians 3:12-13

If we are not serving each other and putting the needs of others before our own (Philippians 2:3-4), then we are not serving God the way we should. If we are truly seeking God and growing in Him, we will be transformed. The love of Jesus will control us and will continue to shape us into the image of our Creator, putting to death the desire to serve self and placing in us a longing to serve and lift up each other. Many times the people in our ministries, especially in the worship ministry, can fall into the trap of competing with one another and trying to "outshine" each other, instead of striving to compliment one another. We tear down rather than build up and we divide rather than unify. We must strive for peace and unity (Heb. 10:24) as we serve alongside each other each week. The enemy would want nothing more than for us to look nothing like the Church while we are serving the church. We have to be intentional about encouraging our teams to serve, encourage, support, and seek to lift up each other and it starts with us. The leader is there for the team, while the team is there for the leader.

Serve the Church

"So then, as we have opportunity, let us do good to everyone, and especially to those who are of the household of faith."
Galatians 6:10

Every ministry in the church exists to fulfill the vision of the church. Therefore, we exist to serve the church and its people. The church doesn't exist to serve as a venue for us to play in, but rather a vessel to shine the light of Christ to the community (Matt. 5:14-16). Many times the demographics of our congregation call for us to sacrifice some of our personal styles and preferences for the sake of ministering to our people right where they are, instead of where we want them to be. This doesn't mean we can't play the new songs and rock out with a band. It just means maybe not right now. It doesn't mean we can't turn the lights down and add stage lighting during worship. It just means not right now. We have to be willing to lay aside ourselves and walk with our congregations as we lead them. On the other hand, meeting them where they are at doesn't mean not challenging them. We must understand that serving the church doesn't mean just giving them what they want, but it means giving them what they need. More than the need to hear that hymn or the newest worship song, they need Jesus and sometimes giving them what they want can prevent them from getting what they need. We have to pay attention to our congregations and serve them in a way that will build trust and confidence, because without these, they will not follow.

Grow

"And he gave the apostles, the prophets, the evangelists, the shepherds and teachers to equip the saints for the work of the ministry, for building up the body of Christ..." Ephesians 4:11-12

Growth is the evidence of life. We discussed this idea back in week 1 when we learned that God is life. All things find their purpose and meaning in Him (Rev. 4:11) and wherever He is, there is life; and wherever He isn't, there is death. Therefore, spiritual growth in our ministry should be a reality if God is at the center. We should see those serving alongside of us growing and maturing, not only in their skills and abilities, but more importantly, in their faith. We should see more evidence of selflessness than selfishness. We should see more humility than pride. We should see more holiness than sinfulness. We know that God's will is ultimately our sanctification (1Thess. 4:3). Just as we are being sanctified by God's power and grace, so are the people in our ministries and if we neglect to disciple and pour into those nearest to us, we are failing to leave an impact after we are gone. What Jesus is doing in their lives should be more important to us than how well they perform.

We must be obedient in following the example of Jesus and duplicate ourselves. First, we must recognize those in our ministry who God may be calling to step out and lead. It is our job to identify these individuals like Jesus identified His disciples (Matt. 4:19) and begin to invest in them. Secondly, we must begin actively discipling them. Discipling doesn't mean just teaching scripture, though that is a big part of it. To truly disciple, we must put our lives on display and let those we are teaching into our world, much like Jesus did. Jesus and

His disciples went everywhere together and every situation they faced was an opportunity for Jesus to teach them. Finally, we must train and equip those we are discipling by giving them opportunity. Many times, people learn better by doing instead of hearing anyway. We can't have such a strangle hold on our ministries that there is no room for anyone else. Experience is the best teacher.

We only have a limited time to influence and equip those in our ministry and we do not need to waste it. Jesus only had 3 years with His disciples and in that time, He equipped them to change the world through Him. One day we will be gone, but will our ministry live on? The heart of a Gospel-centered leader is this: from his first day on, he is planning and preparing for his last.

Go

"For not only has the word of the Lord sounded forth from you in Macedonia and Achaia, but your faith in God has gone forth everywhere, so that we need not say anything." 1 Thessalonians 1:8

When Jesus came to the earth, He had a mission. That mission was to save His people from their sins (Romans 4:25) and lay a foundation of righteousness and holiness that His Church could follow and build upon through the guidance and direction of the Holy Spirit. He confronted a culture of sin and godlessness with confidence and power. He challenged the acceptable norms of the day (Matt. 5:2-7:27) and condemned those who were using their religion as a means to show their righteousness and superiority. He performed miracles (Matt.

15:29-31) and taught so profoundly (Matt. 7:28-29) that people were constantly amazed and overwhelmed. He did not come to embrace the culture He was in, but He came to change it. His influence and impact was so great that people are still being transformed by it today! His message was revolutionary, His presence was bold, His pursuit was resilient, and His faith was unshaken. However, He chose not to do it alone because He knew that the Gospel needed to continue, even in His absence.

The last commandment Jesus gave to His disciples was to *"Go therefore and make disciples of all nations, baptizing them in the name of the Father and of the Son and of the Holy Spirit, teaching them to observe all that I have commanded you." (Matt. 28:19-20)* "Going" can be one of the hardest things to do. It takes us from our comfort zones and exposes us to rejection and failure. It can often reveal our weaknesses and highlight our fears. "Going" means leaving behind what is sometimes safe and expected, and stepping out into the unknown only to trust God with the results. "Going" means being the light of the world and letting that light shine before others (Matt. 5:14-16). It means getting out of the boat and walking on water (Matt. 14:29). It means seeing that *"the harvest is plentiful, but the laborers are few." (Luke 10:2)* "Going" means denying ourselves and taking up our cross (Matt. 16:24) and being compelled by the love of Jesus (2 Cor. 5:14). "Going" is God's plan for His message of hope, redemption, and restoration through Jesus to spread throughout the world. Raising up leaders and sending them out was one of the goals of Jesus' ministry, and therefore, should be ours as well.

Because Jesus went and left heaven to die on the cross for the sins of the world, salvation is a reality for sinners. Because

Jesus made disciples and sent them out, we have the opportunity to hear about it today. It is our responsibility as leaders to not only make disciples and raise up leaders, but to send them out. Jesus sent out his twelve (Matt. 10:5) and He sent out the seventy-two (Luke 10:1) for the purpose of maximizing His impact on the culture and strengthening the faith of His followers. Our impact on our culture has nothing to do with the measure of our skills and abilities, but rather, it has everything to do with if we are sending out leaders. We can be sure that if we choose not to raise up and send out disciples, not only are we not following the example of Christ, we are choosing not to leave an impact for future generations to build upon.

Discussion

1) Discuss any moments of challenge, conviction, or encouragement during this week's lesson.

2) In scripture, we see that Jesus' earthly influence, or ministry, only lasted about 3 years; however, His impact is still going strong. If your ministry, or moment of influence, were to end right now, would your impact die with it? Would your ministry crumble because you aren't there to do everything? Or, would it thrive? Would it continue in your absence because you have equipped others to lead?

3) Many times we are hesitant to let those we are leading have opportunities and responsibilities because we feel that their failures will reflect directly on us. How does it change your perspective when we see all the times that Jesus' disciples failed? Read these passages and discuss. (Matt. 14:30-31, Matt. 26:40, Matt. 26:75, Mark 8:32-33, Mark 9:17-18) We have to get beyond ourselves and begin to see more of the big picture. Jesus knew that the failures were serving the purpose of equipping His disciples to one day step out on their own and not fail. Failing isn't in making mistakes, failing is not learning from them.

4) We must take the words of Paul to heart when thinking of discipling, equipping, and sending out leaders who will be taking our ministry and impact further into the world. He tells us to *"entrust to faithful men"* in 2 Timothy 2:2. Discuss the qualities you would look for

in someone whom you were going to leave your ministry to. Why are these qualities important to leaving an impact?

5) One of the reasons many churches aren't impacting their communities with the Gospel is because they don't have God sized goals. They continue to reach for only what they know they can accomplish. Its leaders are scared to dream big and "get out of the boat". If we are only showing people what we can do, how will they ever see what God can do? List out some God-sized goals that you would love to see Him accomplish and discuss.

Take Away: The Gospel impact of our ministry should be felt long after we are gone. We should be sowing and investing in people today that will be future leaders and influencers tomorrow.

Summary

Hopefully, by now we have realized that leading worship is more than just playing songs. It is living a lifestyle that brings glory and honor to God. It is more than just putting on a production or a service for the sake of meeting. It is about humbling ourselves and serving those around us. Leading worship goes much deeper than inspiring a congregation with our gifts and talents. It is about teaching them about God's character and equipping them to live lives of worship on their own. Worship leading is not about taking or receiving praise from men, but it is about giving praise to none other than Jesus Christ. If we are not careful, we will begin leading out of these misunderstandings that our enemy has created to hold our worship hostage. This study was designed to help us see through the fog of misconceptions and disillusionment and gain greater clarity by looking into God's Word about what our role looks like. We are called to be sober-minded (1 Peter 1:13) as believers and as leaders. We must seek guidance and direction from His Word, instead of the world, if we want to continue being good stewards of all God has entrusted us with.

Worship leading is ultimately about being good stewards. It is about being faithful and maximizing every gift that God has given to us. It is about seeing the worth and the value of the gift while constantly acknowledging and exalting the Giver. It is about intimately knowing God and His nature and character. It is about having a firm foundation of solid doctrine that we can build a lifestyle of worship on. It is about understanding that we are nothing more than tools that God is using during this moment in time to bring people to Himself. Worship leading is about doing the most with what we have been given and striving to be seen as trustworthy (1 Cor. 4:1-2). It is about using our influence to make Him famous (Psalm 115:1) and leading with vision and clarity. Finally, worship leading is about discipling and equipping others to be sent out to lead future generations and continue impacting the world for Christ.

We must always strive for excellence while keeping the bigger picture in mind. It can be so easy for us worship leaders to get used to operating in the moment instead of building for the future. The weekly demands of putting together an excellent worship set can keep us from raising up and training up other musicians and many times, we use excellence as our excuse for not building up others. However, excellence is not merely defined as what happens as the product of our Sunday morning services. Hopefully by now we have learned that there is a much bigger plan at work here. God is redeeming His people back to Himself. He is shaping and purifying our hearts so that we can love Him and worship Him more. So excellence isn't just in the product, it's in the process. It's not always found in the moment, but in the movement from one place to another. With that in mind, let's look at this passage in 1 Corinthians 3:10-11 and examine our hearts.

"According to the grace of God given to me, like a skilled master builder I laid a foundation, and someone else is building upon it. Let each one take care how he builds upon it. For no one can lay a foundation other than that which is laid, which is Jesus Christ."

Meditation

A) Do you see your position of influence and leadership as a gift of God's grace like Paul does, or do you feel as if you have earned it? If by God's grace, then you are a steward. If by your hard work, then you are an owner. Read 1 Corinthians 1:26-29.

B) In what areas of your ministry are you *"laying a foundation for others to build upon"* and in what areas are you not? Why or why not? Is investing in something that you may not see the fruits of important to you? Why or why not?

C) Is selfishness or laziness getting in the way of you *"fixing your eyes on eternal things" (Col. 3:1-2)* and working to equip and empower others so that they will shine when your moment of influence has passed?

D) What other areas of your life are getting in the way of you being a faithful steward of all that God has given you?

Prayer Time

A) Pray that God would forgive you for seeing your talents and accomplishments as something other than a gift from Him.

B) Pray that God would forgive you for occasionally using these gifts for lifting up your name and building your kingdom instead of His.

C) Pray that the Holy Spirit would help you become a better steward of your calling, your gifts, your influence, and your impact.

D) Pray that God would reveal those in your ministry that He wants you to begin discipling and equipping.

Works Cited

[1] Walter A. Elwell, ed., *Evangelical Dictionary of Theology*, 2nd ed. (Grand Rapids, Mich.: Baker Academic, 2001), 496.

[2] Millard J. Erickson, *Christian Theology*, 2nd ed. (Grand Rapids, Mich.: Baker Academic, 1998), 324.

[3] R. C. Sproul, *The Holiness of God*, 0002-Revised and Exp ed. (USA: Tyndale House Publishers, Inc., 2000),

[4] Walter A. Elwell, ed., *Evangelical Dictionary of Theology*, 2nd ed. (Grand Rapids, Mich.: Baker Academic, 2001), 730.

[5] Millard J. Erickson, *Christian Theology*, 2nd ed. (Grand Rapids, Mich.: Baker Academic, 1998), 494.

[6] A.W. Tozer, *The Pursuit of God*, 1st WingSpread Publishers ed. (Camp Hill, PA: WingSpread Publishers, 2007), p.14

[7] Walter A. Elwell, ed., *Evangelical Dictionary of Theology*, 2nd ed. (Grand Rapids, Mich.: Baker Academic, 2001), 1103.

[8] Harold Willmington, "The Origin of Sin," in *The Doctrine of Sin* (Lynchburg, VA: Liberty Home Bible Institute, 1987), 17.

[9] Harold Willmington, "The Origin of Sin," in *The Doctrine of Sin* (Lynchburg, VA: Liberty Home Bible Institute, 1987), 18.

[10] Millard J. Erickson, *Christian Theology*, 2nd ed. (Grand Rapids, Mich.: Baker Academic, 1998), 633.

[11]Millard J. Erickson, *Christian Theology*, 2nd ed. (Grand Rapids, Mich.: Baker Academic, 1998), 720.

[12] Walter A. Elwell, ed., *Evangelical Dictionary of Theology*, 2nd ed. (Grand Rapids, Mich.: Baker Academic, 2001), 502.

[13] Peter Jeffery, *Bitesize Theology: an Abc of the Christian Faith* (Auburn, Mass.: Evangelical Press, 2000), 29.

[14] Bob Kauflin, *Worship Matters: Leading Others to Encounter the Greatness of God* (Wheaton, Ill.: Crossway, 2008), pg. 35.

[15]"The Baptist Faith and Message." *Official Website of the Southern Baptist Convention*. Southern Baptist Convention, 2000. Web. 16 Jan. 2014. <http://www.sbc.net/bfm/bfm2000.asp>.

[16] Piper, John (1995-01-01). "Christian Hedonism Forgive the Label, But Don't Miss the Truth". Desiring God. Retrieved 2014-01-16.

[17] Noble, Perry. *word press*. john bishop, 08 July 2012. Web. 16 Jan. 2014. <http://joshbishopsc.wordpress.com/2012/07/08/newspring-sermon-notes-july-8-weird-week-8/>.

[18] Packer, J.I. *Concise Theology: A Guide to Historic Christian Beliefs*. N.p.: Tyndale Publishers, 2001. Print.